·BIRDS·
ON *THE MOVE*

·BIRDS·
ON THE MOVE

A Guide to New England's
· Avian Invaders ·

NEAL CLARK

Illustrations by
Lucia deLeiris

NORTH COUNTRY PRESS • UNITY, MAINE

LIBRARY OF CONGRESS
Library of Congress Cataloging-in-Publication Data

Clark, Neal, 1950–
   Birds on the move : a guide to New England's avian invaders / by
Neal Clark ; illustrations by Lucia De Leiris.
     p. cm.
   Bibliography: p.
   ISBN 0-945980-04-3 (pbk.)
   1. Birds—New England.   I. De Leiris, Lucia.   II. Title.
QL683.N67C58   1988
598.2974—dc19   88-15216
                                                    CIP

Cover illustration by Lucia De Leiris.
   A Snowy Egret (*Egretta thula*) approaches a saltwater marsh.
Cover and book design by Abby Trudeau.
Range maps by Bruce Hedin.
Edited by Tim Loeb.
Typesetting by Camden Type 'n Graphics,
   Camden, Maine.

Contents

Dedication

To the memory of Ken Rubin (1948–1984),
a friend, forester, and sauntering birdwatcher
of the North Country.

Acknowledgements

The author gratefully thanks the following individuals and organizations who helped see this book through: all the kind folks who contributed their birding adventures; Camp Chewonki, in Wiscasset, Maine, for early encouragement and stimulation; the Harris Center for Conservation Education in Hancock, New Hampshire, for later inspiration; and special kudos go out to Eleanora Cappa, my outdoors sidekick, for being such an all-around good sport.

The New England range maps were drawn by my friend, Bruce Hedin, in the spring of 1988, using available data and the author's personal experience. Although they were done as accurately as possible, they are only meant to show where the individual species are most common. Deviations are to be expected, especially in future years. Any gross mistakes, however, rest with the author—not the map-maker.

Foreword

Through the centuries, New England has been invaded by such diverse entities as the British, blizzards and hurricanes, acid rain, and coyotes. Birds are also invaders, for they fly into new domains altering the food chain and ecological balance in an ever-changing environment. Our lives are a bit brighter now that cardinals, for example, flash around our yards where just 30 years before they were totally absent. Birds are unusual invaders because for the most part they're welcome.

The various general theories of avian range expansion are: the passage of time, habitat changes, availability of food, human assistance, and the weather. Perhaps the Earth's climate (now in a warming, interglacial period) is the most important influence on birds on the move—past, present, and future. It is not within the scope of this book to probe the complicated systems responsible for altering global weather patterns, but basically carbon dioxide build-up in the lower atmosphere may continue to raise temperatures until the next glacial period sets in. Until then more numbers and species of birds could conceivably drift our way.

Birds are more than pretty, flying singers. They are adaptable opportunists who move in, and out, of an area responding to changes in local conditions. New England is fortunate to have all these new—and old—feathered faces scattered around the wooded countryside. The heterogeneous terrain, and conscientious land ethics, are conducive to supporting varied birdlife. From Bridgeport to Brunswick, birdwatchers can anticipate even more variety in the decades to come.

This book is an up-to-date, anecdotal guide to 27 species of birds that have increased their numbers and/or expanded their ranges in New England—most of them during the past 50 years. It is not designed as a field guide (although field guidelines are provided); rather it is meant to inform and entertain readers with interesting facts of natural history and human history, interspersed with birding stories from people across the region. The author also includes fragments of his own journal entries, here edited for brevity, coherence, and continuity. If readers are enlightened, amused, or encouraged to further pursue their birding interests, this book will have achieved its purpose.

Herring Gull

Larus argentatus

The ubiquitous "sea gull" is the largest gray-mantled species breeding in the East. It is so common, so widespread that A.B.C. Whipple, a Nantucket journalist, is pushing for the herring gull to replace the bald eagle as our national bird. "If there's a non-endangered species in the United States today," he said, "it has to be the sea gull. They've learned to live from the detritus of our society. I think that the sea gull would have been a better choice." Most people probably wouldn't agree, but it must be noted that gulls *are* familiar, adaptive, and handsome, smooth flyers. Admittedly they're scavengers, but so are eagles. Whipple faces an uphill battle; bald eagles are coming back from oblivion, a triumphant return from DDT woes. And everybody loves a winner.

Surely herring gulls aren't popular around the Smith and Wesson Company in Springfield, Massachusetts, however; in the fall of 1984, at its golf driving range, gulls bombarded stunned employees with many-colored golf balls. The birds swiped an estimated 500 balls and dropped them around the neighborhood—as they would clams—before company officials closed the range. Logically, the gulls mistook the balls for food, but who's to say they weren't playing a game of their own?

Field Guidelines

The herring gull, 23 to 26 inches long, is white with a gray back, black wingtips, and flesh-colored legs. Its beak is yellow, sporting a small orange dot at the tip, which the young peck when begging for food. First-winter birds are brown, becoming paler in the second and third years on their way to adulthood, which can take up to four years.

Birdbanding, practiced by licensed ornithologists who sex, weigh, measure, and tag over two million birds a year in the United States and Canada, is helping to show where birds winter, where they breed, and how long they live. A banded herring gull is on record as having lived for 28 years; it is one of the longest-lived wild species.

Herring gulls are notoriously vocal. They chuckle, bark like seals, and utter loud, familiar cries that pierce through pounding surf and the somber booms of foghorns shooting through saltspray. Aside from inhabiting ocean beaches, however, they also frequent farms, dumps, and freshwater lakes in search of fish, crustaceans, mollusks, and just plain swill. The only substantial vegetable matter they consume is blueberries.

At herring runs such as Stony Brook in Brewster, Massachusetts, herring and black-backed gulls indulge in feeding orgies each spring as the alewives swim up from Cape Cod Bay to inland ponds to spawn. The fish move by day when the water temperature is right, but it's suicide for many; the waiting gulls tear off heads, gouge out eyes, and gulp down foot-long fish whole. Considerable loss results from this carnage, but enough fish survive to reproduce and return to the sea in September.

Gulls mainly eat dead fish (and have a curious habit of dragging dry prey to the water to soak before eating), but they *can* plunge after live prey like terns, although not from as great a height. With a wingspan of four feet or more they're able to soar high, and drift forward or backward, in a breeze. Gulls are some of the most graceful flyers around, and the seashore would seem barren without them.

When storms spew clams up on a beach the gulls grab them, rise in the air and release them onto rocks, roadways, parking lots, and, rarely, a startled golfer's head. If this ploy fails, they merely fly higher and repeat the process until the shells crack open. Gulls are not, however, feathered Einsteins; sometimes they let the clams go above sandy beaches. The shellfish industry looks upon gulls ambiguously because even though the birds do a number on clams, they also eat moon-shells (beach snails) that drill into clams by the score.

Marco Restani, who worked at the Concord and Manchester, New Hampshire, landfills for the U.S. Fish and Wildlife Service during the summer of 1983, trapped, tagged, and released 250 herring gulls to observe their movements between dumps. "They were crazy about chicken parts," he says. "They could recognize the chicken trucks immediately. They're pretty sharp. I saw a number of them, though, wearing plastic six-pack holders, and a lot of dump birds were one-legged because of broken glass." Gulls, resourceful and ever-ready to live off our waste, confront the hazards of industrial society just like us.

Infanticide is an odd trait appearing in some of these gulls. Adults—sometimes parents—rap chicks on the back of the head until they die. Whether this is done out of competition,

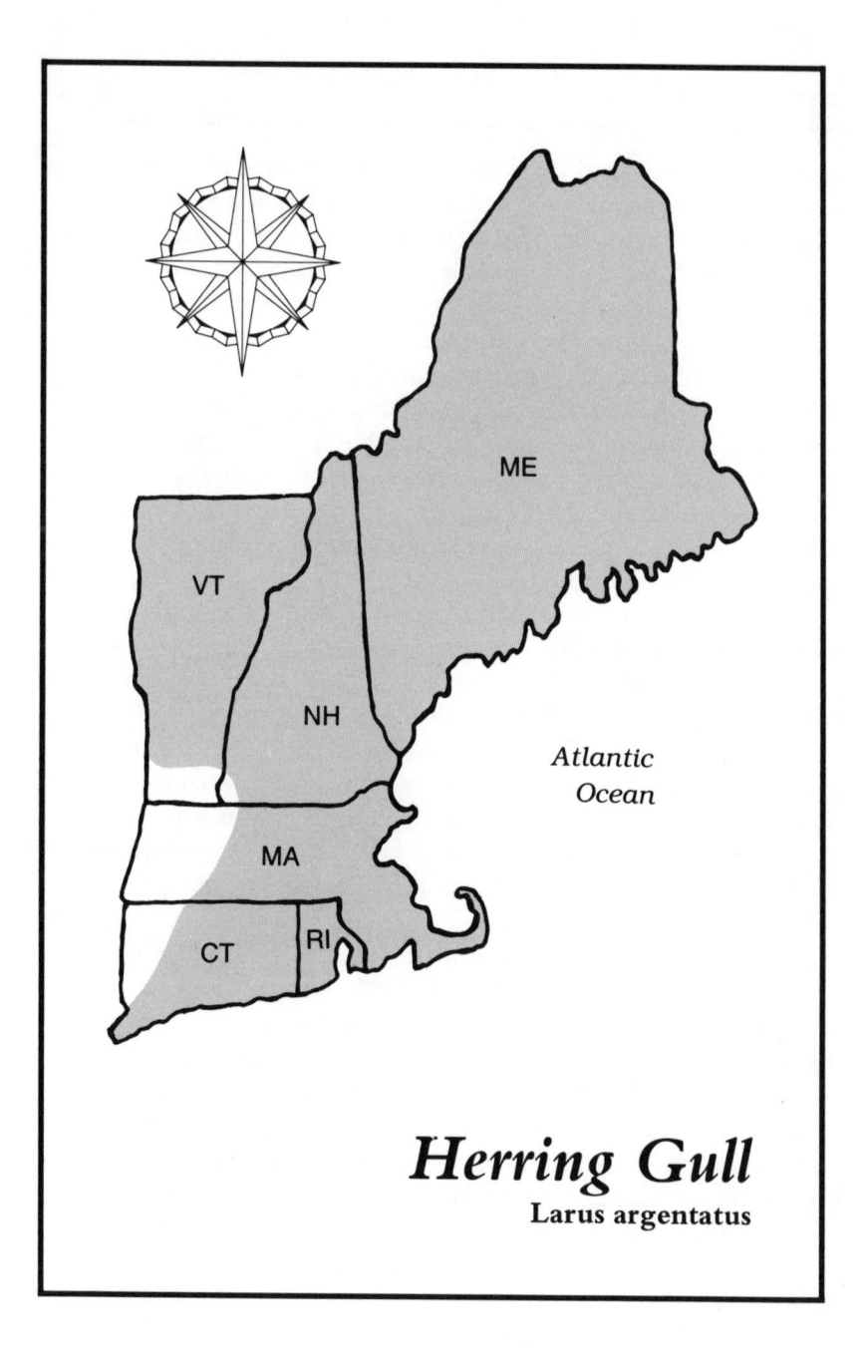

Herring Gull
Larus argentatus

anger at begging young, or only to reduce the population remains a mystery . . . and probably always will. The fact is that several years ago in the Straits of Mackinac, Michigan, 69 per cent of young gulls died, mostly from infanticide. Chicks that wander are murdered for their false steps, making way for those with a better sense of direction.

Herring gulls breed in colonies on the ground, rocky ledges, occasionally on gravel roofs of mill buildings and boat-houses, and, when formerly persecuted by man, in coniferous trees. Breeding territories, usually 30 to 50 yards across, are utilized year after year by the same flock. Males begin the nesting season by competing for sites, pulling grasses in a tug-of-war near territorial borders, and fighting beak and claw. Shortly before egg-laying, pairs raise their bills upward in a courting stance, then copulate.

Nests are made of seaweed, grass, moss, and sometimes feathers and human debris. Parents take on a defensive attitude around their claims, as Major Ralph Mayer discovered on Great Duck Island, Maine, in 1913: "I have repeatedly seen them drive sheep from the vicinity of the nest. On two occasions I was charged by the birds. They did not touch me, but would swoop down at me until 15 to 25 feet from me, when they would go up almost vertically and circle back, repeating the performance. When passing overhead they would utter their piercing 'kee-ew.' "

From his notebook he added, "This is one of the most wonderful sights I have ever witnessed. The air is literally full of gulls. In sight there must be at least 4,000, and all screaming. It is a weird sound. The air is so full of them that it looks like a snowstorm." During the breeding season, the birds are so noisy they can serve as foghorns; boaters know that land looms ahead when they hear the constant clamor slicing through the briny mist.

Conservationist Annette Cottrell experienced more than mere noise, writing in 1984: "A number of years ago, we took our grandchildren out to the Isles of Shoals off Portsmouth. My direction was along a southerly path which led to a gull colony. I hesitated about disturbing the gulls' site, but led on by the opportunity to observe nesting conditions at such close quarters—just a few steps farther . . .

"At this point I was made aware of one gull's alarm call rising above the general clamor; hoarse, rhythmic, as she swooped down on me and up. They had done this on a Penobscot Bay island; it was a signal to go no farther. As I took one more tentative step forward to observe the nestling emerging from its egg, the mother plummeted straight down onto the top of my head—clump—with claw or beak weighted by heavy body force. As the gull raked off, I felt blood running down my forehead. Never had I been so submitted to NO. Rather dizzily, I rejoined my family—good object lesson to the startled children: wear a crash helmet if one must intrude. Better yet, respect privacy."

Mike Zettek also confronted irate gulls, but made a game of it, as seen in his account. "During nesting season, Gull Island, on Narragansett Bay, became at times the focus of boyhood waterfront shenanigans. What more dastardly way to tease an unsuspecting younger brother, sister, or cousin than to row out to the island with the victim, cry 'shipwreck,' and then watch with glee as the raucous herring gulls put on an awesome aerial performance. While I sensed no real danger from the apparent attack, the terrified tykes must have feared for their eyes, or lives, judging from the screams. I would relent and row away to safety before both defensive birds and offensive parents were at my neck."

The usual clutch of three olive-brown, spotted eggs is laid any time from May through August, although June is preferred. Both sexes incubate the eggs for about 25 days after the last egg is deposited, relieving each other every couple of hours. The nestling phase lasts only a few days, but the young don't fledge for about five weeks, during which time the parents bring in swallowed food, bow their heads, and regurgitate on the ground or into cavernous mouths.

U.S. Fish and Wildlife official A.O. Gross studied a colony of 23,000 gulls on Kent Island, New Brunswick, in 1940, recovering 773 banded birds. First-year birds were found, on the average, 1,380 km from Kent Island; second-year birds 695 km; and third-year birds ventured only 495 km. In general, then, younger birds dispersed much farther than their elders—a phenomenon called nomadism which can be explained by the younger birds being more adaptable and better equipped to wander greater distances.

Population and Range

Herring gulls were scarce in New England at the turn of the century, following years of persecution: eggs and young were eaten by man, and feathers were prized in the millinery trade. Dealers paid 40 cents per adult and 20 cents per immature bird— no pittance for the times. On a bridge between Boston and Cambridge, officials stopped the shooting only because horses were bolting at the gunfire. Back then there were an estimated 5,000 breeding pairs along the New England coast as far south as Penobscot Bay, Maine. Soon, however, due to changing fashions (long-plumed hats mercifully went out of style), and Maine's islands becoming depopulated, the gulls returned in unbelievable numbers. Legal protection, coupled with accessible human waste in open-pit dumps, has also aided the gulls' comeback, a comeback that's been met with both smiles and frowns.

The first record of nesting in Massachusetts following protection was in 1912. By 1930, herring gulls had started a massive takeover of Muskeget Island in Nantucket Sound. At that time, laughing gulls held the island, numbering approximately 20,000, but by the 1970s fewer than 100 remained. The larger, more aggressive herring gulls had ousted their little cousins. The question is will black-backed gulls displace the smaller herring gulls as both species spread southward at alarming rates?

Maine's breeding gull population had exploded to such proportions by the 1930s that the U.S. Fish and Wildlife Service instituted a poisoning program. From 1940 to 1952, 900,000 eggs were sprayed with oil and formaldehyde—the oil to suffocate the embryos, and the formaldehyde to prevent the eggs from rotting so that incubating parents felt all was well beneath them and wouldn't lay again. The overall population did not decline significantly, due to the longevity of the species; while there were fewer young being born, the adult population hadn't been cropped. If the program had continued a few more years, it might have been more effective with natural die-offs eventually decimating the adults.

The spraying campaign temporarily stopped the increase in Maine's flocks, but by then the prolific, opportunistic gulls had already invaded the Bay State. There was no halting the advance. By 1955 herring gulls bred in Chesapeake Bay; in 1958 they hit Virginia; 10 years later they reached the North Carolina coast, which is the current southern limit of their range. They also breed in Alaska, Canada, around the Great Lakes, and across the North Atlantic. They're increasing worldwide, but they may soon reach their expansion potential in the Northeast. Their successful day at the beach is bound to darken and end.

The most widely publicized gull control program in recent years took place on Monomoy National Wildlife Refuge off Cape Cod, where the Massachusetts Audubon Society tried to manage the dwindling tern population. Short-eared owls, black-crowned night herons, floods, and human interference, in addition to herring gulls, which usurp prime nesting sites and prey on the chicks, have reduced tern numbers. In recent years about 50,000 gulls have nested on Monomoy Island, but only about 7,000 terns, so the Massachusetts Audubon finally relented and cooperated with the U.S. Fish and Wildlife Service's management plan. In 1980, federal biologists left cubes of bread spread with poisoned margarine in herring and black-backed gull nests. (Terns don't eat bread.) Roughly 2,000 gulls died of uremic poisoning, but after only one of three proposed baitings the Society withdrew its support of the program due to negative membership reaction. In 1982 a couple hundred more gulls were shot because they wouldn't vacate the tern nesting areas, and a year later officials fired air cannons and shotguns loaded with firecrackers in the area before the terns returned for the season. Also, some gull eggs were smashed. These measures have had minimal impact on the terns, and even less on the gulls. Simply put, some species are making it and some aren't. Terns don't appear strong enough to combat marauding, robbing gulls, even though ornithologists are on their side.

Herring gulls have also been creating a ruckus at airports. Showing a preference for warm resting/loafing areas, they often choose runways, where the surface temperature can be 10 degrees centigrade above the ambient temperature. This results in birds colliding with planes, and getting sucked into jet engines on takeoffs. Birds have caused airplane crashes for decades, and aviation officials are so concerned that Bird Patrol personnel now keep constant vigils. With herring gulls spreading south, new problems arise at each infiltrated airport. At Logan International Airport in 1983, Allen Counter, a Harvard professor of neurology, found that gulls can lose their hearing from jet roar, which might explain why the birds fly into planes. Scarecrows, firecrackers, and air cannons, once a good defense, are becoming useless deterrents against the deaf gulls.

• *Journal Notes* •

June, 1980

The Isles of Shoals, eight little islands belonging to both Maine and New Hampshire, lie 10 miles southeast of Portsmouth. Today I visited Appledore Island, where Cor-

nell and the University of New Hampshire operate the Shoals Marine Laboratory, a teaching facility and research center. As I landed at the dock, gulls were in the air and on the ground, yet itching was on my mind; besides harboring the largest herring gull colony in New England, Appledore is prime poison-ivy country. I stepped gingerly around the glistening green bushes and bird nests, picking up a few gull pellets—those one- to two-inch balls of indigestible matter that are regurgitated several hours after predatory birds feed. The pellets I dissected contained the usual fishbones and crabshells, but also glass, paper, aluminum foil, and rubber bands. Gulls eat absolutely anything, whether it's edible or not.

I learned that 2,224 pairs of herring gulls are nesting here this summer, and nearly 4,000 pairs on the eight islands combined. I thought it ironic that 80 years ago gulls were being saved as part of the first conservation movement in the East. Now, these wily birds are too numerous, forcing us to choose between gulls and terns. Overpopulation breeds rage not only among the individuals involved, but also among their protectors. When the dust settles, I hope we humans have made the right choice. The best action would seem to be no action. Let the birds fight it out between themselves. We'd do well to steer clear and remember Darwin.

May 28, 1983

While canoeing with John Thompson on Lake Massabesic, New Hampshire, we found one of New England's southernmost breeding loons on a wooded island. Then we approached an incubating herring gull on a boulder in the water. The bird flew off the side of the rock, revealing a nest of pine needles and sticks . . . and three eggs, size extra large. Bones, droppings, and pellets covered the foul-smelling site, which intrigued both of us. (Most naturalists I know relish pawing through dump trash and wildlife spoor.)

We landed on a small island and immediately found another gull nest, hidden beneath some winterberry holly, three blotched eggs in the clutch. We didn't linger; ground-nesters face enough trouble from a myriad of predators. I wish more people would respect families other than their own—such as lowly herring gulls.

Snowy Egret

Egretta thula

This, the only white heron-like bird with black legs and yellow feet, helped establish the National Audubon Society.

During the 19th century, breeding plumes (aigrettes) of white herons were sought by the millinery trade for women's hats, and by 1903 hunters were paid $32 per ounce, making the feathers worth literally *twice* their weight in gold (if the equivalent relationship existed today an ounce of these feathers would be worth over $800!). The shooters simply watched the birds' flight lines to their rookeries, and made easy kills. Eggs rotted and nestlings starved. The 50 or so plumes on each egret's back

drove men money-mad; white meant stacks of green. The plun-
der became so intense that in 1905 Audubon warden Guy Brad-
ley was gunned down as he attempted to arrest poachers caught
in the act of killing four egrets in Florida. His body drifted in his
boat until found the next day by boys who noticed vultures
soaring overhead.

The National Association of Audubon Societies (now National Audubon), which was incorporated that same year to
stop the slaughter of herons, gulls, and terns along the Atlantic
coast, was aghast at the murder. So was the rest of the country.

The Audubon Society circulated pamphlets and lobbied
Washington, demanding full protection for all plumed birds.
Then the millinery trade spread a story that only shed plumes
were being retrieved from the rookeries—that herons and
egrets were not touched. Anyone who believed that lie never
saw the hundreds of stiff, soiled bodies among the mangrove in
what is now Everglades National Park. The snowy egret came
closer to extinction than its relative the great egret because it was
less wary and its shorter, delicate plumes were in more demand.

In 1913 the National Association of Audubon Societies
lobbied successfully for a clause tacked onto the Tariff Bill to
halt the importation of wild bird plumage into the U.S. This
action was followed by the signing of the Migratory Bird
Treaty, whereby federal protection was afforded transitory species. The U.S. Biological Survey (later the U.S. Fish and
Wildlife Service) immediately outlawed spring shooting, set
seasons and bag limits on waterfowl, and prohibited the killing
of shorebirds other than woodcock and snipe.

Egrets were on their way to a slow, sure recovery. Looking back, it's difficult to believe the ruthless carnage for mere hat
trimmings, but such were the styles and the times. Perhaps
remarks made by U.S. Senator James Reed of Missouri best
evoke the selfish ignorance of the era. In 1913 he said, "I really
honestly want to know why there should be any sympathy or
sentiment about a long-legged, long-necked bird that lives in

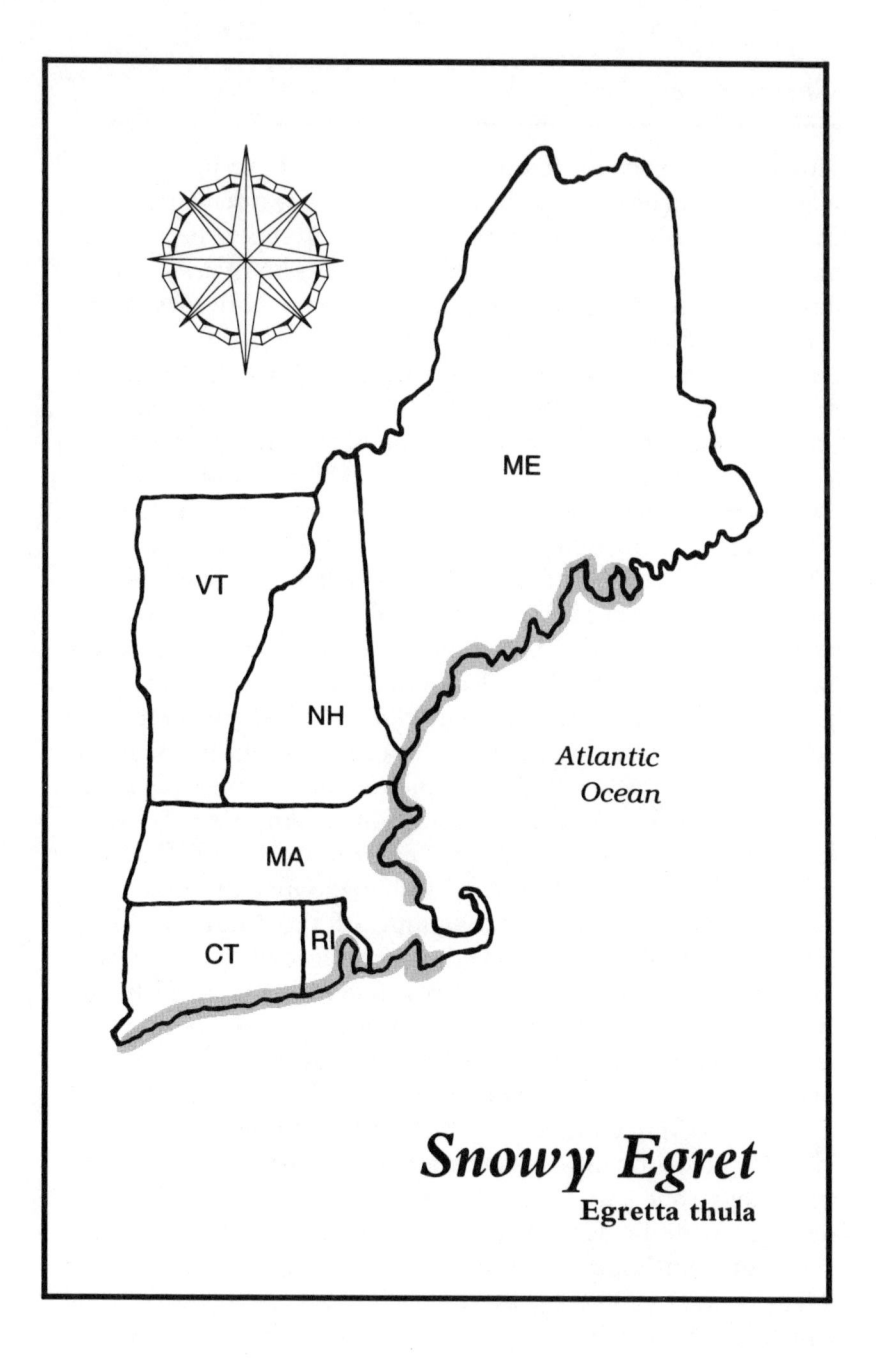

ME

VT

NH

Atlantic
Ocean

MA

CT   RI

Snowy Egret
Egretta thula

swamps, and eats tadpoles and fish and crawfish; why we should worry ourselves into a frenzy because some lady adorns her hat with one of its feathers, which appears to be the only use it has?"

Field Guidelines

Slightly larger than a crow, the snowy egret is indeed snowy; it's pure white with black bill and legs, with striking yellow feet visible when it high-steps through the water. Calls are harsh croaks, generally heard only during the breeding season.

Snowies are shufflers, thrashers, waders of fresh and salt water. They congregate at ponds, swamps, and marshes, adding a touch of the tropics to New England tidal flats, their cottony forms reflecting in cold, teeming pools.

Mike Zettek, a naturalist from New Hampshire, even found these birds near the big city: "I got to really know snowies the summer of 1980, when I worked on Thompson Island, one of the Boston Harbor Islands. Located only three miles from the Massachusetts capitol dome, and less than a mile from the J.F.K. Library, the 100-acre island has two salt-marshes—a rarity in the Boston area. I would guide visitors on walks, and could always count on showing off at least a half-dozen egrets. I never tired of steering visitors to a hideaway in some planted pines where we could all be birders—binoculars or not—and watch for slow motion yellow feet moving in the mud, or the lightning-fast bill spearing a fish; and this with Boston's skyline in the background!

"I also love the photo of a space shuttle liftoff at Cape Canaveral with a snowy egret taking wing in the foreground. That is a powerful image of hope, for me."

John James Audubon described the egret's diet and feeding habits in 1840: "The snowy heron, while in the Carolinas, feeds principally on shrimp. Many individuals which I opened there contained nothing else in their stomachs. At a later period, they feed on small fry, fiddlers, snails, aquatic insects, occasionally small lizards and young frogs. Their motions are generally quick and elegant, and, while pursuing small fishes, they run swiftly through the shallows, throwing up their wings." (Readers should understand that America's most famous bird artist—the man whose name is synonymous with wildlife conservation—often shot dozens of birds as models for a single drawing. He chose to use freshly killed birds instead of stuffed specimens, and didn't have to rationalize his shooting; birds were everywhere in those days. This was long before spotting scopes, quality binoculars, telephoto lenses, and movie cameras, which allow us to zoom in close without ruffling a feather. He used the limp bodies to show the world how beautiful all birds are. Fortunately for the birds, there are bag limits today, and most modern artists prefer looking at study skins instead of down the barrel of a shotgun.)

Snowy egrets nest colonially with other egrets and herons, sometimes by the thousand. They build their nests in marshes, rice plantations, and on the mangrove islands off southern Florida. According to the American Littoral Society, half the original wetlands in the Lower 48 have been polluted or developed (for houselots, landfills, or dumps), rendered useless to living things. Additionally, about 90% of all saltmarshes on the East Coast have been ditched to control mosquitos. Wetlands are important to humans for water supply purification, and flood control, but no less vital to wildlife. They're the richest and most diverse of habitats. Out west large freshwater marshes are still numerous, but in the East, such ecosystems are much reduced. The long-legged waders rely on saltmarshes, where tons of organic matter are produced per acre per year—twice as much as the annual yield of the most fertile field.

The egrets usually nest below a height of 12 feet in trees and bushes, often selecting cedars where available. Nests are flat, loosely-made platforms of sticks, taking about a week for both mates to build. When the mating urge strikes, male snowies squawk, raise their crests and aigrettes, and strut around the females in graceful courtship prances.

Annette and Bill Cottrell, two veteran birders from Hillsboro, New Hampshire, recall a trip to a huge colony in Louisiana: "When my husband and I visited the McIlhenny Sanctuary in April, 1962, we had in mind Olin Sewall Pettingill's estimate of about 30,000 birds nine years before. As we approached on foot that large artificial island, the sight that greeted our eyes was almost unbelievable. To find a long pier with an observation tower built right into the middle of the lake seemed too good to be true. As we settled ourselves down with binoculars, we noticed other wooden structures dotted about where egrets could build their nests. So ensconced in our eyrie, we were surrounded by clouds of diaphanous white birds pursuing their life cycle with a sense of concentrated energy that was awe inspiring."

Females lay three to five bluish eggs in April or early May, and 18 days later the babies hatch into a world of fog, sun, and waving, feathery reeds. During extreme heat parents shield their nestlings with half-spread wings. The parents feed them by regurgitation, and adult birds sometimes vomit on human intruders, too—the most fetid "acid rain" imaginable. Young birds fledge in about 25 days but stay close to home, returning to the nest nightly until wanderlust hits and they forsake the rookery forever.

Snowy egrets and other long-legged waders have a habit of wandering northward in late summer following nesting. Whether these meanderings—often covering hundreds of miles—are warmups for spring migration, a method of population dispersal, or merely a search for better feeding grounds, no one is sure. People in northern New England and the Maritimes know, however, that when snowies glide in from the South, and monarch butterflies prepare to leave for Florida, a new season is arriving on roving wings.

Population and Range

At the beginning of the century snowy egrets were accidental drifters to New England, headed toward extinction. They bred only as far north as New Jersey, and then only sporadically. The first breeding pair colonized Massachusetts (on Martha's Vineyard) in 1962, followed by a gradual range expansion north along the coast. In this country, the current breeding range runs from Florida to Bar Harbor, Maine. Northern birds tend to nest singly or mixed with other herons, not in large rookeries. On certain islands, however, such as the Isles of Shoals off Portsmouth, New Hampshire, and House and Clark Islands near Plymouth, Massachusetts, 200 to 300 active nests are tallied annually.

With total protection and changing ecological views, the species should continue to radiate northward. Wetlands are the key. As long as there are extensive salt marshes, snowy egrets will fish and nest among the Spartina grasses as living symbols of modern conservation ethics.

• *Journal Notes* •

September, 1982

I'm gazing across the 3,000-acre Scarborough Marsh, the largest salt marsh in Maine, and my heart is pumping pell-mell. It's dusk, and I've just watched eight snowy egrets fly in from Pine Point, necks folded, seemingly all wings. They glided in a line, silently, and dropped into the water. White elegance in knee-deep mire.

Whenever long-winged, slow-flapping birds like geese and egrets pass, they leave me in a state of agitated envy. I yearn to fly in their company and see the earth from an airborne perspective. Scarborough Marsh isn't the Everglades, where herons abound like shorebirds do around here, but it sure does the trick. Just count my heartbeats.

Cattle Egret
Bubulcus ibis

This recent arrival to the Northeast—and North America—is the only white heron with an orange bill and legs. The specific name, "ibis," was the name of a sacred Egyptian bird that resembled a stork.

Less than 40 years ago American birders ventured to Africa's great grassy plains just to check this species off their life lists. There, alongside cattle, elephants, and water buffalo, birders watched egrets wiggle side to side, and strike at insects rousted by the beasts. Now, following one of the most explosive range expansions in history (and the first time a species has come here from the Old World under its own power . . . and prospered), birders don't have to leave the region; cattle egrets breed in all six New England states and are increasing even where there's no cattle. The white birds have adapted extremely well to our continent, and without ousting any natives. The cattle egret is a model immigrant that's here to stay.

Field Guidelines

Dressed in pure white, cattle egrets sport buff-colored feathers on the crest, chest, and lower back during the breeding season. At this time of year they croak gutterally, as somehow befits the heron family, a group of long-legged waders and skulkers of swamps, marshes, and black lagoons.

Unlike other members of the family *Ardeidae,* however, the cattle egret prefers farmland and damp fields to real wetlands. Wherever livestock abounds (especially in Florida), the egret is sure to follow. Literally. Alongside tractors, too. And when beast or machine stops to rest, so too does the egret.

Thelma Babbitt wrote about the egret's feeding behavior in foreign lands: "The first time I ever saw cattle egrets was in 1963 as I was driving with a friend through cattle country near Mandeville, Jamaica, West Indies. I was so startled to see those large, pure white birds with yellow bills among a herd of Holsteins. They stood out so clearly in the lush green grass in the pasture. We stopped the car and with binoculars watched them closely. In spite of their name, it didn't occur to me they would actually be so closely intermingled with those large animals, but as we watched, it was obvious why. They kept just in front of the cows and caught grasshoppers which were disturbed as the cows fed.

"I saw them again in 1971 some 10,000 miles from Jamaica. That spring I was in Amboseli Game Park near the border of

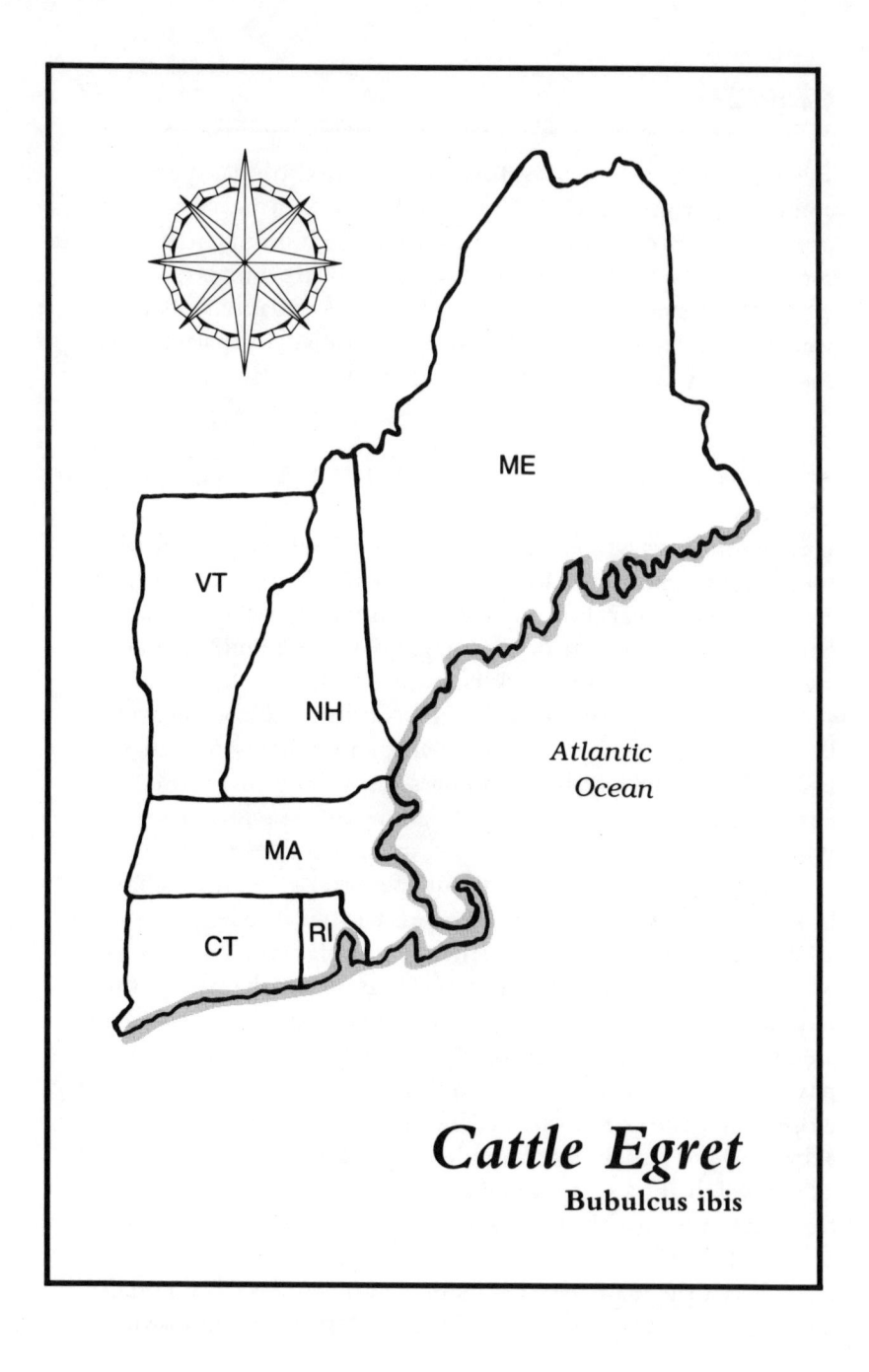

ME

VT

NH

Atlantic
Ocean

MA

CT   RI

Cattle Egret
Bubulcus ibis

Kenya and Tanzania, almost in the shadow of majestic Mt. Kilimanjaro. There are big herds of water buffalo there—huge, ferocious beasts with massive horns on their foreheads. To my amazement, there were dozens, if not hundreds of the stunning white cattle egrets, catching insects as the buffalos grazed. And some egrets were roosting on the backs of the animals, flying down periodically for a meal. They stood out starkly white in contrast to those black animals. For some reason, they seemed only to be with the water buffalo—not with the large herds of zebra, wildebeest or gazelles. Why?"

Also fond of amphibians and fish, the egret is a peerless opportunist, having swept into unfamiliar terrain, sought out ancestral habitats, and made off with the goodies. It doesn't even have to work very hard for a living. The patient bird simply waits for a commotion to put insects to flight, and then wolfs down easy pickings. The very stance of the egret connotes an aura of quiet cunning and confidence, similar to a house cat waiting by the refrigerator, knowing the door will soon magically open. It's a serene yet alert posture that exudes a tough, new-kid-on-the-block image, except this newcomer isn't tough. The cattle egret is only testing old traits on a new continent. And adjusting extremely well.

In buttonbushes, cedars, and maples egrets build stick nests up to 25 feet above the mire. They live colonially, and the whitewash-spattered nests are often only a few feet apart. Three to six bluish white eggs are laid, incubated by both parents for three weeks, and by mid-summer the fledglings disperse and wander toward Florida. There they winter at their favorite feeding grounds: the cattle country of the Sunshine State's interior.

Population and Range

The coming of cattle egrets to this country is one of the most celebrated avian invasions in recorded history. Unlike starlings, house sparrows, and house finches, the egrets were not brought here in cages and released; they arrived unassisted. Despite the fact that two of the first individuals were shot, they've been welcomed by birders and farmers alike.

In the 1920s egrets spread from Africa and Asia to South America, and from 1930 to 1960 they ranged 2,000 miles up to the central United States. Texan birders recorded 10 pairs in 1959, but by 1966 the count soared to 20,000 pairs. Their current breeding range includes the entire Eastern Seaboard as far north as Nova Scotia and New Brunswick inland to the Great Lakes. In its winter range, however, which includes the Gulf Coast and Florida, the population has been mysteriously dwindling since about 1971. Weather, a reduction in available land, or a combination of the two could be responsible. The U.S. wintering population might be reaching its carrying capacity.

The fascinating story of the taking of the first North American specimen is best told by Allen H. Morgan who, along with Richard Stackpole and William Drury, participated in the chase:

"Any white heron in Massachusetts in the month of April, 1952, was unprecedented, and instantly made that birding expedition a 'red-letter day' the moment we spotted it. But as it focused in our binoculars we were dumbfounded: we had no idea what it was despite our close familiarity with all herons native to North America. It *had* to be collected, an urgency which cannot be appreciated by anyone not schooled in field ornithology by Ludlow Griscom, Jim Peters, et al. We had the necessary permits, but not the hardware. While home and firearms were only two miles distant, we desperately feared the bird would fly away. The farmer with whose cows the bird consorted produced an ancient shotgun, and shells even older. We approached the bird—which was not particularly wary— and the trigger was squeezed. Despite considerable smoke and noise, the charge barely cleared the muzzle, and the egret flew off over the horizon.

"Frantic pursuit by auto proved fruitless. We could not find the bird, and an opportunity to add a new species to the North American checklist was fading. Drastic action was called for. Why not an air search? A good friend nearby had a small plane, and we could be in the air searching the region in an hour. We were, and soon spotted the bird with another herd of cows less than a mile away. A regular pattern developed: shot at in herd #1, the bird flew to herd #2 followed by me in the aircraft; shot at in herd #2, the bird immediately returned to herd #1. While adequate firearms and ammunition had been acquired in the meantime, the bird was becoming wary, and so closely intermingled with the cows as to require use of a rifle. After six or eight round trips between the two farms, the bird finally fell to Dick Stackpole's 10th or 15th shot; he was a far better ornithologist than marksman! The egret was finally in hand, and clearly—from the condition of plumage and feet—not an escapee. Our elation was heightened even more when we met Griscom and his party within minutes of the bird being secured . . . but what a disappointment for them. Almost totally lost in the excitement of that morning was our first ever for the Sudbury Valley: glossy ibis and upland plover. What a day indeed!"

Readers who question the ethics of killing the prize bird must realize that (as cruel as it seems) ornithological tradition requires first individuals of a species new to an area be collected. That Sudbury cattle egret was the first on the *continent*. Admittedly, however, it's ironic that dedicated birders are forced to kill. The specimen in question is preserved at Harvard University.

The story doesn't end there, though: it was later learned that a month before the Sudbury bird was spotted Boston Red Sox photographer Richard Borden had unknowingly taken pictures of cattle egrets in Florida, assuming they were snowy egrets. And, in the fall of 1952, there was another Massachusetts cattle egret, seen on Cape Cod, which was shot by a local hunter. Reports soon came from New Jersey and elsewhere, and the first known nest was discovered in a heronry on Lake Okee-chobee, Florida, in May, 1953.

How the first individual came to this country is unknown. It's surmised that trade winds aided the feathered explorer as it crossed the Atlantic from West Africa to northern South Amer-ica—a distance of about 3,000 miles. From there it was a mere hop, step, and flap over Cuba to Florida and on up the coast, touching down for a short-lived glimpse of springtime in the Bay State.

Cattle egrets found an unoccupied niche here, and proba-bly won't force our native herons out because the newcomers breed later and nest in slightly different habitats. Plus, they're not overly aggressive. We'll continue to see these legal aliens as long as we remain beef eaters and milk drinkers.

• *Journal Notes* •

July, 1975

A day off from Park Service ranger work at Cape Cod National Seashore. I habitually headed to the Provincetown dump, where human and avian scavengers root about. The herring and black-backed gulls were in seventh heaven on piles of succulent trash, and as I watched through binoculars I caught a flash of saffron. There, perched atop shiny kitchen appliances, I focused on a cattle egret, an uncommon tramp that also picked over the seaside swill.

Glossy Ibis

Plegadis falcinellus

This is the only ibis species likely to be found in New England. The generic name, "plegadis," comes from the Greek, meaning scythe, which refers to the shape of the bird's curved bill.

When Franklin Roosevelt was President, and Lou Gehrig and the New York Yankees were repeatedly winning the World Series, the glossy ibis was seen mainly in Florida. It rarely strayed as far as the Northeast, and then only for brief stop-overs. Annette and William Cottrell, from New Hampshire, recall the excitement of their first sighting: "In the early '30s, we

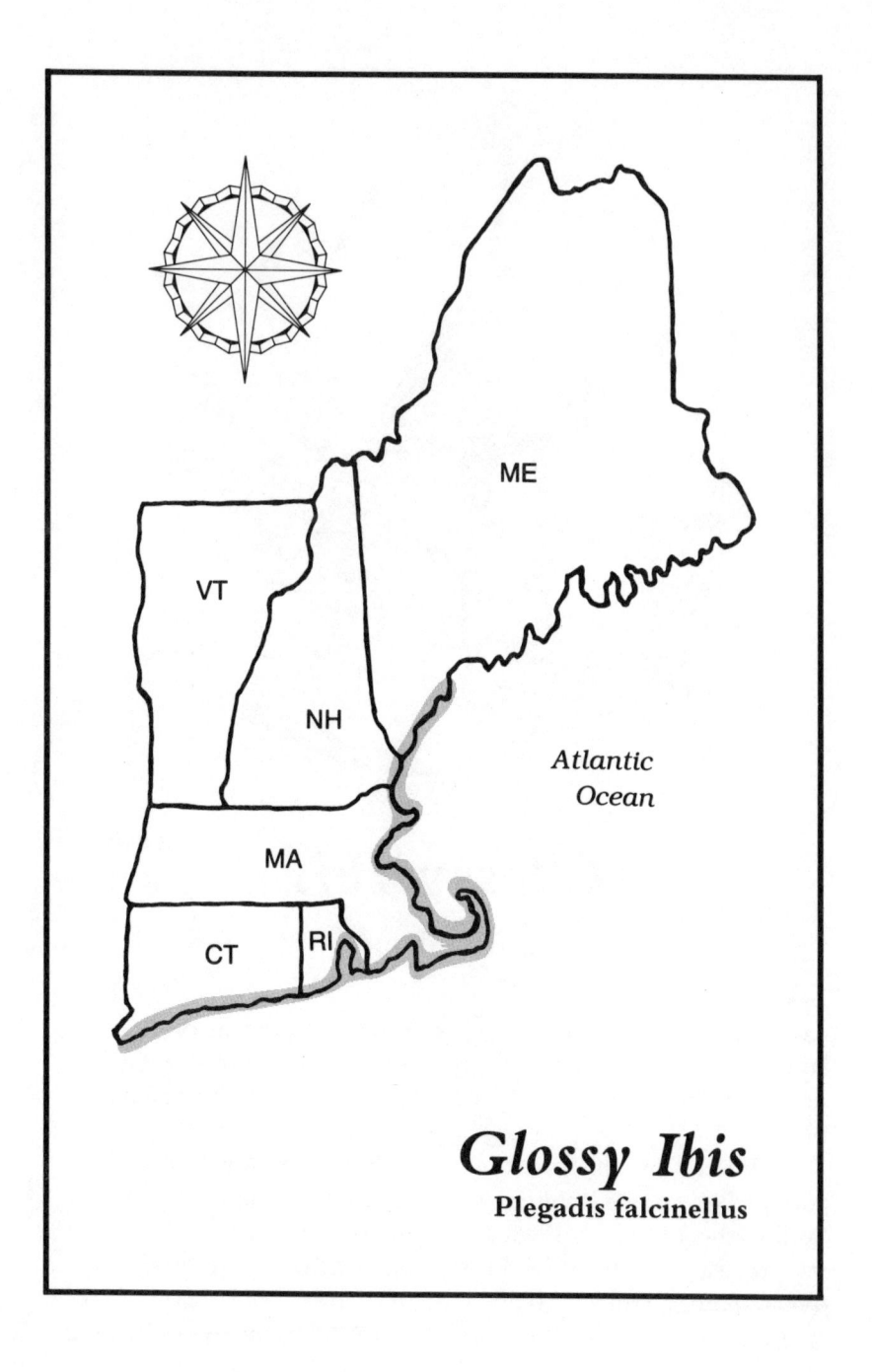

ME

VT

NH

*Atlantic
Ocean*

MA

CT RI

Glossy Ibis
Plegadis falcinellus

moved to within a block of Mount Auburn Cemetery in Cambridge, Mass., where we learned to climb the high fence and get in a couple of hours of birding before breakfast. As the most favored spot in the region, we came to meet other birders—easily spotted with their binoculars, slow pace, and abstracted eye. Among them was a short, square man wearing a formal business suit and fedora hat, no matter what the weather. His air of authority bred respect. Like lowly house sparrows, we picked up the crumbs of gossip.

"About the middle of the month, we were electrified by the news that a glossy ibis had just been seen on Plum Island. A bird new to the region and so exotic! On the third report that the bird was still there, Bill urged me to telephone the square man (Ludlow Griscom, field ornithologist at Harvard's Museum of Comparative Zoology) to get exact directions. I remember his courteous voice and clear directions: 'You know Hell Cat Swamp? Go to the northern edge of the bluff an hour before sunset. Keep low, be quiet, and the bird will fly in from the marshes to roost below you. Good luck. Let me know.'

"An hour and a half's drive to Newburyport, another hour down the sandy track behind the dunes of Plum Island. That had been a favorite picnic site, now assuming a more significant stature. As silently as possible we parked and crept on hands and knees to peer out over the scrubby swamp. No bird. We were in plenty of time and flattened ourselves to watch the sun, setting across the marshes . . . and endure the mosquitoes. The rhythmic wash of waves on the beach persisted inexorably in our ears as we cautiously shifted to a more endurable position as one, then two hours passed. It was getting cold, too. Well, it was a good try. In tacit agreement, we stood up, shaking out the stiff cramps, raising arms to stretch.

"At that moment, a dark shape swept up silently below us and headed out across the now-dark-crimson sky. The long scimitar bill extended from the slender body and trailing legs, as its wide wings flapped, deliberately. This was the silhouette of the primordial, extra-terrestrial being that we had been almost sitting on, and, thank heaven, it deigned to give us a look. Our first encounter looms most happily in memory."

Now, some 55 years later, the species breeds up the East coast to the Maritime Provinces, without the fanfare of the cattle egret. It just quietly found its place and multiplied.

Field Guidelines

Ibises are long-legged waders with great decurved beaks, and the glossy is aptly named; it shows shiny purplish feathers up close, black at a distance. Standing fully two feet tall, it flies with neck extended (unlike a heron), and legs trailing behind a fanned tail. The wingspan exceeds three feet.

Calls are gutteral grunts, sounding like a cross between a crow's caw and a sheep's bleat. The birds vocalize mostly at the nest and upon landing in roosting trees.

The ibis is a bird of fresh and saltwater marshes, swamps, flooded fields, and tranquil coastal bays. There it hunts crayfish, fiddler crabs, insects, and snakes—usually the poisonous water moccasin which takes scores of ibis eggs. The moccasin, or cottonmouth, ranges north to Virginia only; it's no wonder that ibises have fared so well in New England.

The glossy is a colonial nester, building its stick and dried-plant platforms in the company of other ibises and herons. Nests are placed on the ground or in semi-aquatic trees up to a height of 10 feet. The ibis has an unusual homemaking trait: all during incubation and beyond, the parents keep adding nesting material. (Most other birds completely finish nest-building before the eggs are laid, and don't bother adding more material.)

Oscar Baynard, in Arthur Cleveland Bent's *Life Histories of North American Marsh Birds,* wrote of a pair's affection that he witnessed in 1912: "They stand erect and seem to rub their bill against the other one, all the time making cooing (gutteral, I must admit) notes of endearment, preen each other's feathers, and act just like a couple of young humans on their honeymoon. These loving scenes continued until the young were able to fly, never seeming to diminish at all. This trait I certainly admire, and while it is known to exist in birds that mate for life, is seldom seen in birds that are supposed to mate for only a season."

In April or May the female lays three or four "robin's-egg blue" eggs, which hatch in 21 days if cottonmouths or fish crows don't eat them first. Oscar Baynard continues his anthropomorphic notes on ibis nestlings: "I never noticed the young fighting among themselves, but at all times they acted like well-behaved children, the only exceptions being that the three older birds would often take turns in trying to swallow the last hatched baby. He was sure a hardy scamp or he would never have lived through the treatment. When the young were over three weeks old, over half the food would be moccasins. I kept a record of the food by making the young disgorge after the old ones had fed them. I spent usually eight to ten hours a day in the blind photographing and making notes, and no day during the four weeks did the parents make less than six trips each with food for the young, and they made on some days as high as 11 trips each, the last ones being late, sometimes after dark." Today's ornithologists do not have to resort to such tactics in checking diets. They dissect pellets and carcasses, but they don't induce vomiting. Such were the old ways of dedicated—yet often cruel—birders.

Population and Range

In the spring of 1850, there was a major influx of ibis to Connecticut and eastern Massachusetts, but until about 100 years later they were still only sporadic spring visitors. Slowly they extended their breeding range northward; by the 1960s they reached Rhode Island, and by 1973 they colonized Clark's Island off Plymouth, Massachusetts. At about the same time, ibis invaded Appledore Island near Portsmouth, New Hampshire, where they have maintained 25 or more nests ever since. By the late 1970s Maine's Scarborough Marsh also harbored the birds, along with the already-established herons and egrets.

Although glossy ibis are not common breeders in New England they are no longer considered "exotic" as Annette Cottrell remembers them half a century ago. They are now local nesters in coastal colonies, and will thrive and increase to the carrying capacities of fragile marine environments. The sole question mark regarding their future is the situation in the West Indies, where many of them winter. There, disturbances at nesting sites, and the usual problem of habitat loss and poisons could combine to decimate New England birds, thus abating the expansion. Until that time ibis will grace our skies and shores with a touch of the tropics.

• *Journal Notes* •

April 17, 1982

A blustery, vibrant day at Plum Island. I heard the first spring peepers of the season, and, above the observation tower near Hellcat Swamp, saw nine glossy ibis. They flew in a straight line about 50 feet overhead, one behind the other. For an instant I had the urge to reach up and try stroking the shining feathers, but resisted the absurd temptation—content gazing agog at these birds that were so rare here when I was born.

Common Loon

Gavia immer

The common loon, also known as the great northern diver and hell-diver, is the only loon with a dark head and bill that summers in New England.

Northern New England's most celebrated species since about 1970, the loon makes steady newsprint, appears on Audubon emblems, and once was the background star of a major motion picture: *On Golden Pond*. (The birds' images and haunting cries, the latter previously recorded in Maine by professor William Barklow for his 1980 album, *Voices of the Loon,* framed the elderly couple's summer.) Although not increasing at the rate of, say, cardinals, loons—thanks to efforts by the

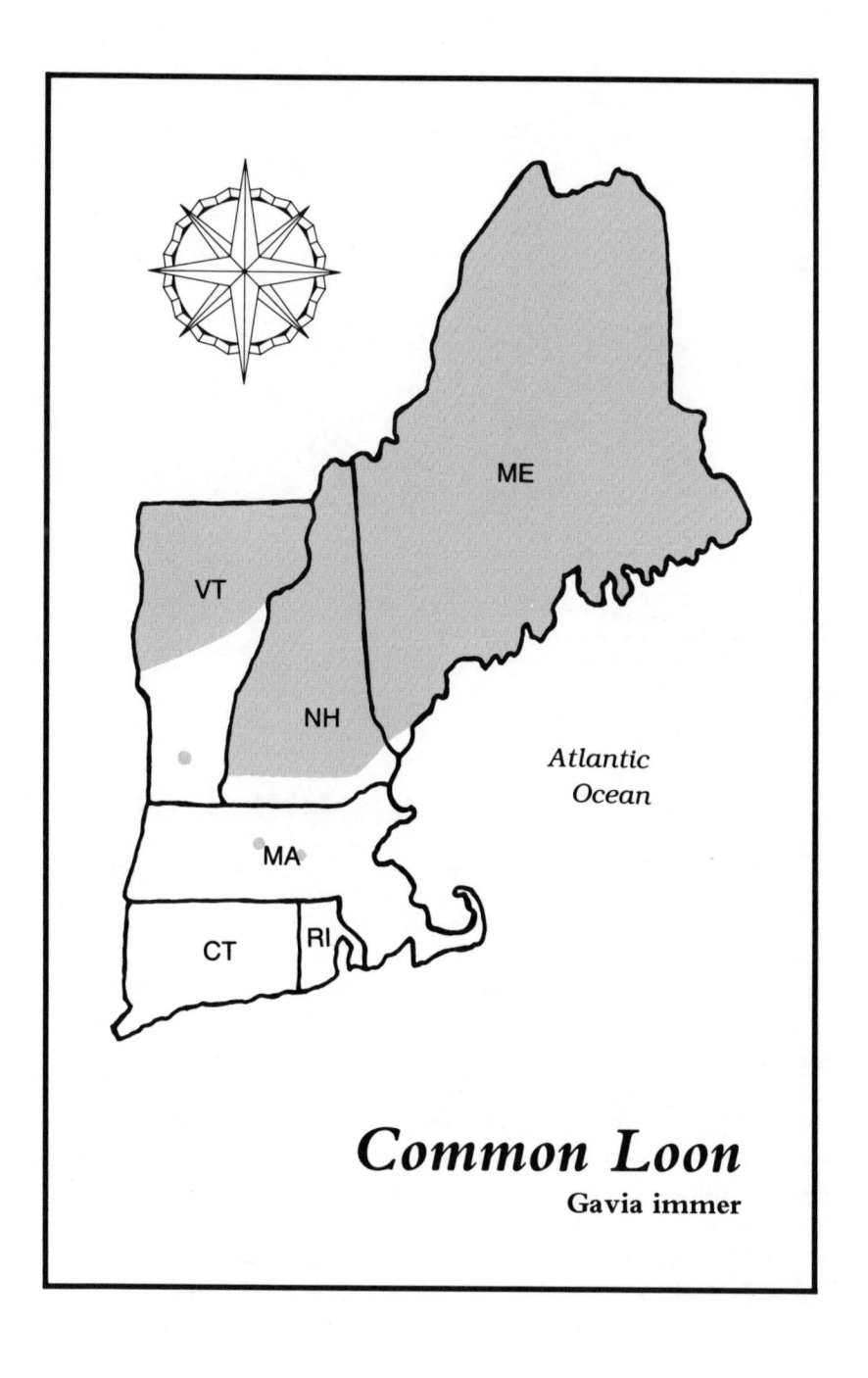

ME

VT

NH

Atlantic
Ocean

MA

CT RI

Common Loon
Gavia immer

North American Loon Fund and New Hampshire's Loon Preservation Committee—are falteringly coming back. After a 70-year absence, they now again breed in western Massachusetts.

In Henry David Thoreau's era, loons nested in eastern Massachusetts, too, and he marveled at their cunning on Concord's Walden Pond: "When I went to get a pail of water early in the morning, I frequently saw this stately bird sailing out of my cove within a few rods. If I endeavored to overtake him in a boat, in order to see how he would maneuver, he would dive and be completely lost, so that I did not discover him again, sometimes, till the latter part of the day. But I was more than a match for him on the surface. He commonly went off in a rage."

Field Guidelines

The common loon is a low-swimming diving bird up to three feet long. It has a sizable, dagger-like beak, a checkered black and white back, and scarlet eyes in summer. It is truly built for diving: the webbed feet are located considerably farther back than they are on a puddle duck for efficiency when swimming, but causing the birds great difficulty when walking on land. Unlike the dabblers, which can spring up from the water like a helicopter, loons need a running start (pattering on the water surface) of at least 100 yards into the wind to take off. On a calm day it can require 300 yards for these six-to-ten-pound birds to rise.

Calls, especially at night, are weird and memorable. The two most common are tremolo giggles or chuckles that resemble gull laughter, and sad, haunting wails that slowly fade from the birds' barely-opened mouths. These wails are heart-tugging strains, connoting the mourning of a lost friend, and echo across a lake, painting the air with misty melancholy. In flight, loons sometimes bark. Astute observers have also noted that loons regularly start calling whenever small airplanes fly over their sacred lakes.

Loons are denizens of deep, freshwater lakes surrounded by wild lands. A 100-acre pond is barely large enough to support most pairs. In winter they're found on the ocean and in coastal bays.

Mainly fish-eaters, loons also take aquatic insects, crustaceans, frogs, and a small percentage of plant matter. They hunt by poking their heads in the water, detecting prey, and then diving, using their wings as well as their webbed feet for propulsion. Loons can remain underwater for fully three minutes, and have been accidentally caught in nets at 200 feet.

Nests are built of grass, reeds, rushes, sphagnum moss and twigs, close to or on the water, and measure about two feet across. They are well camouflaged. Artificial nesting islands, which were implemented in the early 1970s, are anchored offshore for the birds, thus eliminating certain predators and flooding during spring's high water. These floating wooden rafts (lately made of plastic milk jugs and wire) have proven successful; in New Hampshire they now support approximately one-quarter of all the state's chicks. With natural nesting sites disappearing each year in New England, the man-made platforms will be even more crucial in the decades to come.

In April, shortly after icemelt, pairs migrate from the coast to establish territories and participate in courtship rituals, which include wing-flapping, water ballet, and singing duets. They produce one or two thick-shelled, olive eggs and take turns incubating for about 29 days. By the first official day of summer, loon chicks are hatching around central New England, and by early to mid-July in northern regions. Within days they take to the water, and also ride (partly hidden) on the parents' backs for the next couple of weeks.

After witch-hazel's aureate flower show replaces final leaf-fall, and ice forms on inland lakes, most loons fly east to the coast. They circle high on migration, in ones and twos, stopping wherever there's open water. At such a place and time, Villa Ramsay and her husband had a chance loon sighting: "About 7 a.m. one fall Saturday, we took the canoe to Deering (New Hampshire) Reservoir. It was cool, and mist was coming up off the lake. Slowly the sun came over the hills, and, to take advantage of the warm rays, we headed for the far side. While approaching a small uninhabited island, three low-slung forms glided smoothly out in front of us. We both saw them about the same time, stopped paddling, and watched, fascinated, as they swam, dove and called. The mature pair were the first to move away, while junior continued his display. We both agreed it was serendipity."

Population and Range

The common loon was so *un*common in Massachusetts by 1905 that it was considered extirpated. Connecticut supported very few nesting pairs. Much later, Vermont and New Hampshire saw a reduction in breeding birds, while Maine continued to maintain its healthy numbers. The reasons for the gradual disappearing act—long before its wavering comeback—are many, and mankind is behind every one.

In 1970, the Audubon Society of New Hampshire, noticing a steady decline of the loon population, began a statewide survey of breeding families. By 1975, with the formation of the Loon Preservation Committee, such summer-long surveys became even more extensive and accurate. Other New England states followed suit: Maine established the Loon Project in 1977 because of declines in southern sections; Vermont, in 1983, set up a Loon Watch Day. (On July 21, 1984, from 8 to 9 a.m., 129 people checked 109 lakes, and spotted 30 adult loons and 6 chicks.)

The major reason for the loon's initial setback was scarcity of nesting sites. It still is. Summer homes and resorts have sprung up like dandelions, especially in New Hampshire, one of the fastest-growing states in the East north of Florida. Loons are wilderness-loving birds, and upon human intrusion into traditional nesting territories they simply slip off their nests and resettle farther north. Few remain to adjust to this invasion of privacy. Noisy motorboats disturb them, and even canoes (often carrying concerned naturalists) are a problem because they can maneuver close into quiet coves where the birds nest.

Raccoons, attracted to camps and campgrounds, also raid loon nests for the jumbo eggs. The masked marauders have a tougher time, however, reaching the floating rafts. More of these artificial islands could perhaps be installed, but water levels still have to be controlled for other pairs nesting naturally a few feet from shore. Natural water-level fluctuations can affect nesting success, but man-made alterations can be devastating: dams quickly lower levels (forcing loons to travel—clumsily— on land), and also raise them, flooding nests. But where there's cooperation, there's hope. In 1981, Union Water Power Company, which controls the hydroelectric dam on Lake Umbagog on the Maine-New Hampshire border, held water levels within six inches of nests during incubation. Twelve chicks hatched, compared to one survivor the year before. Union Water incurred no significant cost. Also in 1981, on Grafton Pond, New Hampshire, the State planned to lower the pond for dam repairs during nesting season, but postponed the work after learning the timing was so crucial to the loons. Two chicks hatched, again at no extra cost.

Acid rain, which has already made many of New York's Adirondack Park's high-elevation lakes devoid of fish, is a threat to all living things, including loons. According to the Izaak Walton League, most fish die when the pH level of a lake is much below five. No fish, no loons. New Hampshire is particularly vulnerable because her soil is thin and the rock is granitic, lacking lime to neutralize the falling acid. About six New Hampshire ponds are crystal-clear yet lifeless.

Acid rain forms when sulphur and nitrogen oxides are chemically changed to acids in the atmosphere, then blown hundreds of miles, usually east to Canada and New England from the Midwest where they originate. Power plants, smelters, and automobiles are the culprits. Acid rain is a serious, complex issue that won't blow away. It is destined to be the most important environmental problem for the rest of this century . . . or however long it takes politicians to act on regulating emissions. Meanwhile, loons and other fishers still manage to catch their limit.

A newer, equally insidious threat to avian populations befell wintering loons near Dog Island off the northern Florida Gulf Coast in 1983. Dozens of the birds washed up emaciated, dying in the dunes. The loons, anemic and starving, weighed only two or three pounds—a quarter their normal weight. That winter more than 2,000 loons died, from Sanibel Island to Texas. Intestinal flukes and mercury poisoning were suspected, the mercury being accumulated in body fat over years. Afflicted birds lose the instinct to hunt and eventually starve. Mercury poisoning is the latest of several human-caused assaults on these defenseless creatures. Somehow, loons have dived and dodged most bullets, returning to old haunts to reproduce, symbolizing hardy wilderness survival.

The loon's current breeding range extends from the Arctic to western Massachusetts. According to the Maine Audubon Society, the estimated 1985 Maine population exceeds 3,000 individuals—more than seven times all of New England combined. In New Hampshire, where the population and survival rate have increased rather steadily since 1981, the Loon Preservation Committee counted 382 birds on 139 lakes during their one-day loon census in July, 1985, an increase of 30 birds since 1984. Vermont has been experiencing a decline in loon numbers in its southern half, while the rest of the state supports limited pairs; only ten nesting pairs were counted in 1985, although there was a higher success rate among chicks that year.

Loons are once again making it in Massachusetts. According to Bradford Blodget, assistant director for nongame and endangered species in Boston, loons were "firmly reestablished in 1975 and now slowly increasing. In 1984, four pairs had nests on Quabbin Reservoir, and on another reservoir in central Mass., there was a fifth nest. There's a lot of excitement about this. The future is bright, providing no catastrophes occur—like acid rain or an oil spill on the winter coast. I'm not too worried about them, though. They've done it on their own without our help. Loons can take care of themselves. Other areas in the state could possibly support them, too." It is interesting—and ironic—that loons fare rather well on man-made reservoirs. Though not technically wilderness areas, reservoirs are apparently wild enough for the birds' liking. Let's hope reservoirs aren't the only sites available to them by the next century.

New Hampshire's Loon Preservation Committee, which boasts 3,000 volunteers, has made life easier for the celebrated birds. When members discovered that over half the lakes previously occupied by loons had been abandoned by them from 1925 to 1975, they went to work putting up signs to keep boaters away from nests. They also distributed pamphlets and monitored floating rafts and natural nesting sites. Currently they even offer a $100 reward to those who provide information leading to the arrest and conviction of anyone harming a nest, adult, or chick. The group is determined to reduce the species' "threatened" status in the Granite State, but without public cooperation, it might not happen. It's not enough to put out platforms each year; uninitiated people have to be educated to keep away during nesting season. Loons are like antisocial, territorial fishermen: they shun outsiders, and only want to be left alone in their watery world of solitude.

• *Journal Notes* •

May 18, 1983

High Head, Cape Cod National Seashore. Dawn. I just finished walking 20 of the 30 miles of Great Beach, from

Henry Beston's Outermost House to Provincetown. A sight for sore legs: the sun is rising out of the water, orange like a burning coal, beckoning me onward over the sand. Lobster boats are already spanning across the shore, chugging, complaining in a lingering fog. A pair of loons chuckles overhead, beating strongly toward the East, necks drooping, calling wildly. It seems late in the season to migrate, and I wonder if they're headed for Maine or farther north. And I wonder if they'll live out their potential 20 years. Regardless, their calls will echo for decades deep within my mind.

June 17, 1985

Afternoon loon patrolling. I canoed out to a rounded rock at the far end of Wilder Pond and sat with binoculars watching a four-day-old chick and its two parents. After awhile I lost sight of the chick, only to spot it head down, dead. I was dumbfounded. I waited half an hour before retrieving the body; the parents were wailing away, and I wanted to give them grieving time. Finally I moved in and picked up the fuzzy chick, to be sent to the University of New Hampshire for examination. Starvation is suspected. The boulder in the pond—until now unnamed—will be dubbed Dead Loon Rock, in memory of this fallen diver.

December 7, 1985

A loon in winter plumage was rescued from iced-over Wilder Pond today. Ravens had been attacking the floundering bird, and the loon ranger couldn't bear to watch anymore, so he ventured onto the thin ice and captured it with his bare hands. The weakened loon is now recovering in the Harris

Center bathtub. How bizarre it is to hear those wild wails reverberating behind a bathroom door. (The same tub once held a beaver, until it escaped and chewed off the windowsill.)

Mute Swan

Cygnus olor

This is the only species of swan likely to be seen in New England at any season.

Swans figure in history, dating back to the time of Socrates, who told of them singing a sweeter, special song just before dying: their "swan song." Later legends expounded on this, claiming that a mortally wounded swan sets its wings and glides into the water, uttering strange notes. The "swan song," a current metaphor for one's last act (for example, a writer's last story, or a ballplayer's final at-bat), is perhaps mythical. But is it merely an expulsion of air? No one knows, but authoritative

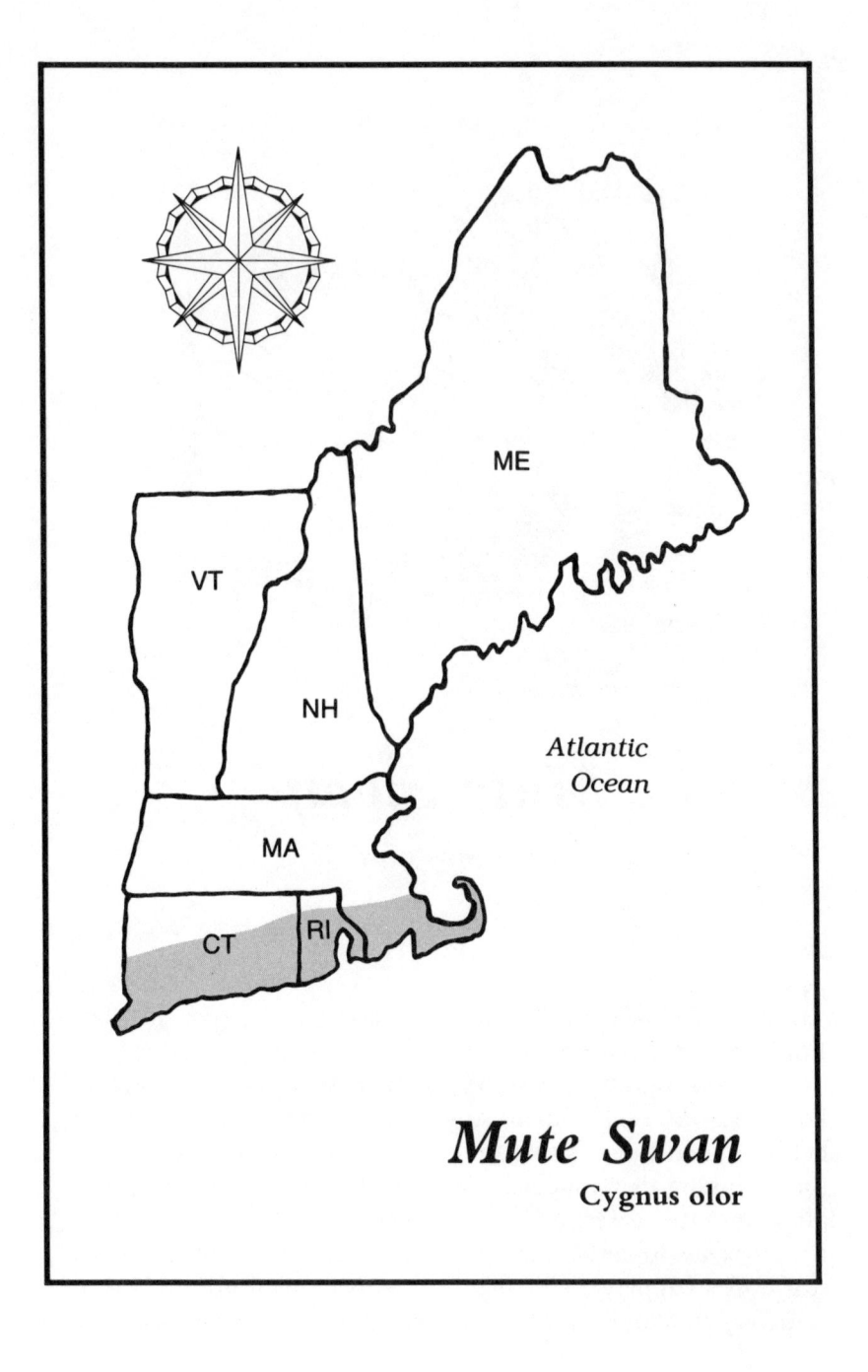

Mute Swan

Cygnus olor

ears *have* heard these weird calls, which are uttered only upon impending death.

Mute swans are of European origin, and have been domesticated as graceful "lords of the lakes" since the 12th century. During the Middle Ages, Englishmen ate these swans, though now they're considered royal; no citizen can legally own one except by special permission of the King. Edward IV declared in 1482, "No person whatever, except the King's son, should have any swans of his own, except he hath freehold lands to the clear yearly value of five marks."

Field Guidelines

The mute swan is white with black legs and a knobbed, orange bill. Usually the bill points downward, and the neck is often S-shaped. Wingspans exceed seven feet. As the common name suggests, this swan is generally silent, except for occasional grunts and hisses while at the nest or attacking.

These are birds of fresh and saltwater ponds, bays, and lagoons—any quiet sanctum with open water and plenty of succulent food. They are root-eaters, and because of their longer necks, they can outreach most other waterfowl. (In 1984, a family of eight swans destroyed a quarter-acre section of cranberry bog on Cape Cod, causing $5,000 damage. Under an agricultural protection statute, the owners legally killed one adult and all the cygnets, or young swans.) In winter, when the birds remain near the seashore, they have to eat more crustaceans, aquatic beetles, and softshelled clams to compensate for the shortage of available vegetation.

Swans, as every park visitor knows, also accept bread—even the cheap white variety. Elliot Taylor reports feeding attempts: "I once fed bread to two adults and five cygnets at Westport, Massachusetts. As I started throwing bread into the 200-foot-diameter pond, they came swimming across and started eating. When my loaf was gone, I bent down to pick up the pieces that had fallen at my feet. I was now in a charging position, and the adult male swan ran out of the pond at me and hit my legs with his breast and wings. I turned and ran about 30 feet and he went back to eating—the clear victor. Be careful with swans. They are big and powerful, and will attack in an instant." (Those who feed birds should be aware that offering their feathered friends free lunches may be harmful to their health: heavy concentrations of waterfowl can suffer from communicable diseases. Also, corn and bread, high in carbohydrates, can be detrimental in springtime, when the birds need more calcium for egg-laying. Well-intentioned people should keep their feeding to a minimum, even in wintertime. Let wild birds fend for themselves, off the dole.)

As Taylor attests, mute swans are aggressive and defensive, and not only near the nest. Rampaging birds have been known to attack canoes, racing shells, children, and they even bite boat ramp tires. When one of these elegant birds fluffs up, throws its neck out and beats it heavy wings, intruders best retreat. Cobs (male birds) have dragged dogs into the water, drowning them. Swans have no natural enemies other than man and the occasional snapping turtle which takes some young. The problem is not protecting the species, it's how to contain the present population in areas where there will be minimal harm to people and property.

Mute swans build large, mound-like nests of cattails and other aquatic vegetation, and line them with a few feathers and down. Nests can reach six feet in diameter, and are placed on the ground near water. Five to ten grayish eggs are laid, depending on the age of the female; older birds lay more eggs. The incubation period lasts five weeks. Mute swans are more prolific than the Arctic-breeding whistling swans, and the aggressive mutes sometimes oust the whistlers at coastal wintering grounds. This is one of the main reasons why wildlife personnel don't always welcome this newcomer as warmly as they could.

Flying swans can match the highway speed limit of 55 miles per hour, and because of this, coupled with their enormous wingspan, many of them collide with power lines, dying of electrocution when both wings touch two wires simultaneously. From 1960 to 1984, conservation officers found more than 320 zapped swans on Cape Cod alone.

Population and Range

In 1910, 216 swans were imported for domestication to selected lavish estates near Rhinebeck, New York. Wealthy Americans, not to be outdone by the British, sought this extra touch of class. Two years later, 328 more came to Long Island. Unlike the practice in England, some of these birds' wings were *not* clipped, and they migrated to warmer areas in winter. By the spring of 1936 swans reached Westport, Connecticut, and a few years later they made it to Charlestown, Rhode Island. So began a northward invasion.

Rhode Island now has a solid population of about 700 birds; Connecticut, from 1966 to 1984, saw its population soar from 300 to 1,400, including approximately 120 nests, according to wildlife biologist Greg Chasko. During that same period Massachusetts swans increased from 100 to 700. Cape Code has also experienced a substantial rise in numbers, and the increase continues: the first swans to come to Salt Pond Waterfowl Sanctuary in Falmouth appeared in the fall of 1960. By 1985, more than 70 birds were permanent residents in that small area.

Mute swans are scarce in northern New England, but considering past history and the fact that London (where swans abound) is on the same latitude as Newfoundland, it's only a matter of time until they colonize the Maine coast. Waterfowl malaria, transmitted by blackflies, seems to be a limiting factor, however. New Hampshire has a very small breeding population, and in Vermont and Maine the species is listed as "rare."

So far. Introduced birds are not always welcomed here in New England, but this species is an exception. Providing they don't overpopulate and drive out wintering Canada geese, they'll have a home on our shores—soft-white reminders of Wordsworth.

• *Journal Notes* •

April 3, 1973. Durham, N.H.

The ice is out of the Mill Pond. Spring peepers and blackbirds alternate calling, all urgently. My old friends Agatha and Hamilton have returned from a winter in Portsmouth. This feral pair of mute swans nests annually on a hummock in the middle of the pond. Soon I'll be leaving the University, but long after I'll remember their stunning beauty and territorial ways. If I return after graduating, I hope they'll still be swimming around the cattails, still the talk of the town.

Killdeer

Charadrius vociferus

The killdeer is a shorebird in the plover family. Its two black breastbands are diagnostic. The specific name, *vociferus,* is an accurate description of this thoroughly noisy bird.

It was formerly a hard-to-hit gamebird, but when farmers and sportsmen learned that the bird's diet consists of over 90% insects, they aimed at more tempting and easier to hit targets. (To "run like a killdeer" is an expression still used in the South.) Today the species is fully protected.

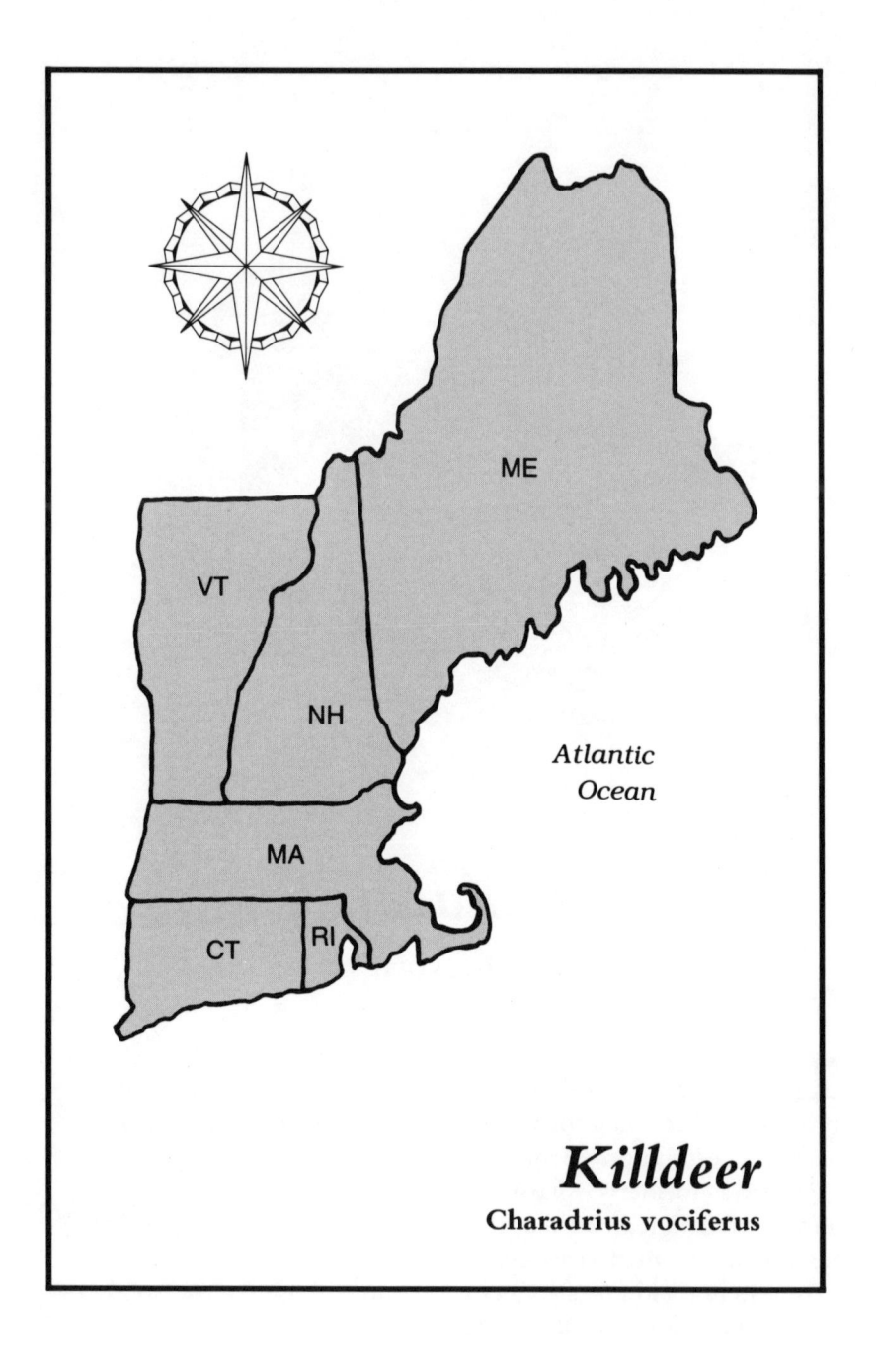

ME

VT

NH

Atlantic
Ocean

MA

CT

RI

Killdeer

Charadrius vociferus

Field Guidelines

Killdeer are spindly-legged, robin-sized birds with brown backs, golden rumps, and two prominent black breastbands. When the birds stand still these bands create an unbirdlike form, serving as a kind of camouflage called disruptive coloration. During World War II the U.S. Army used a similar camouflage technique, concealing big guns, airplanes, camps, etc., with bi-colored nets.

Prowling birders soon learn that killdeer are highly vociferous in the field, especially near the nest. The excited calls of Kill-*dee!* are loud and repeated endlessly. The birds also make persistent, plaintive trillings similar to a spring peeper that jars the nerves yet touches the heart.

Killdeer have benefitted from agriculture in the past, and despite the disappearance of countless farms they're still holding their ground and even increasing in some areas. Not ones to put all their eggs in one pasture, they adjusted to the changing trends of man, and now place them on flat, gravel-topped roofs as well. Commonly inhabitants of fields and mudflats, they've also taken to golf courses, lawns, and airports. Ben Allison writes, "Killdeer will nest anywhere. Around 1976, a pair nested in the middle of the Monadnock Regional High School track, in New Hampshire. This field was used extensively by the kids every day during this late-spring nesting. But, because of the efforts of a strong nature club, the birds remained unmolested and nested successfully." One bold pair even placed a nest on the cobblestone steps of the Atomic Energy Commission headquarters in Washington, D.C.

Aside from their beauty, rapid flight, and running ability, killdeer are valuable economically. Farmers and backyard gardeners are pleased that they eat crane flies, weevils, clover-root curculios, mosquitoes, grasshoppers, wireworms, and diving beetles. Killdeer sleep but little; they are active after dark, hunting for earthworms on moonlit nights.

Unlike other plovers, killdeer typically nest far from water, such as on lawns, ballfields, driveways, sandpits, airport runways, and in cemeteries. Because they need pebbles and gravel to hide the eggs via camouflage, they appreciate flat rooftops, as John Thompson discovered. "One summer, on hiatus from my regular job of teaching high school science, I took a job painting in Bedford, Massachusetts. The second day of work, I was walking across a gravel roof of a school we were painting. My job was the trim in a roof entryway, and I was armed with a four-inch brush and a bucket of white latex. I was stepping over broken bottles, squished softballs, soggy pieces of paper, approaching my assignment, when I spotted her. She was a killdeer, a handsome brownish bird with two distinctive black chevrons on her breast. She saw me, and began to behave rather oddly, running diagonally away from me, dragging her left wing. It was as if she was playing 'tag' and wanted me to catch her.

"I put down the tools of my trade and followed her. She zigged and zagged, keeping a sharp eye out at me, peeping loudly, never letting me get closer than 30 feet, but making sure I was still behind her by cocking an eye at me occasionally. I soon tired of the chase, went back to retrieve my brush and pail, and proceeded to the entryway. She still was trying to entice me with her broken wing routine when I saw the reason for the game: next to an air vent was a small nest with three speckled eggs. I walked toward it. Her peeps became shrill. Not wanting to scare her from the nest, or to place myself in danger of a well-placed peck, I retreated. She didn't return to her nest, however, until I finished my painting and descended from the roof. She was still there a few days later. I assume she raised a family successfully."

Villa Ramsay, a teacher from Deering, New Hampshire, writes that "a killdeer nest was built in our strawberry patch one spring. Typically, each time I approached she'd drag her wing to lead me away from the nest. Those eggs did hatch." This ploy of wing-dragging, tail-fanning, and feigning injury, which is used exclusively around the nest, is effective on predators and sometimes people. Females do it only as a last resort, after camouflage fails. Meanwhile the male careens overhead, berating and harassing the interlopers until they leave.

Killdeer don't actually make a nest, but scrape out a little depression in an open area, sometimes lining it with grass, wood chips, or refuse. Females usually lay a clutch of four pointed eggs in May, the narrower ends facing the center of the nest to conserve space. The spotted, blotched eggs, on a background of assorted drab colors, are well masked, as most birders know. Both mates take turns incubating the eggs for about three and a half weeks. A study conducted in Mississippi during the late 1970s revealed that parents not only shade eggs with their wings to keep them cool, but actually soak themselves in nearby ponds and resume incubating.

Population and Range

The killdeer is a common breeder throughout New England, present from March to October. It is a summer resident from the Maritime Provinces down to Massachusetts, and a permanent resident below the Bay State all the way to Florida. A few individuals winter on Cape Cod, where the population is surprisingly low.

Similar to the nighthawk, killdeer have witnessed the loss of prime open land under the name of "development." But both species seem to adhere to the philosophy of "If you can't beat 'em, join 'em." They quickly altered nesting behaviors, living more closely to our houses simply out of necessity. Killdeer have fared even better than nighthawks, and it's a credit to their resourcefulness that their numbers have not declined during this century of rampant human construction and habitat destruction. Indeed it would not be surprising if killdeer increased their numbers and became even more familiar head–bobbing streakers in cities and towns everywhere. A bird that can nest between the ties of an active railroad track is a bird with a bright future in the 21st Century.

• *Journal Notes* •

May 5, 1984. Hillsboro, N.H.

Blackflies and high flies in left field. While chasing down a softball hit deep during practice, I scattered a pair of skittish killdeer. After I threw the ball in, I happened to notice their four buff and chocolate-brown eggs on the hard-packed dirt. The parents screamed at me all the way to the infield. I marveled at their spunk and the fact that they chose such a heavily-used site. How long will the exposed eggs last? Will the camouflaging work? Birding while competing in sports is a winning combination, but this situation is too close for comfort. When the regular season starts, I'll have to play shallower, and just tip my cap to the new left fielders.

Wild Turkey

Meleagris gallopavo

This uniquely American species is the same one served at Thanksgiving. When the Continental Congress of 1782 designated the bald eagle our national bird, Ben Franklin objected; he thought the eagle was a despicable scavenger and that the wild turkey was the obvious choice.

The Mexican race of turkey was introduced to Europe in the 1500s, and later brought to New England by the English colonists. By the late 1600s, however, due to indiscriminant

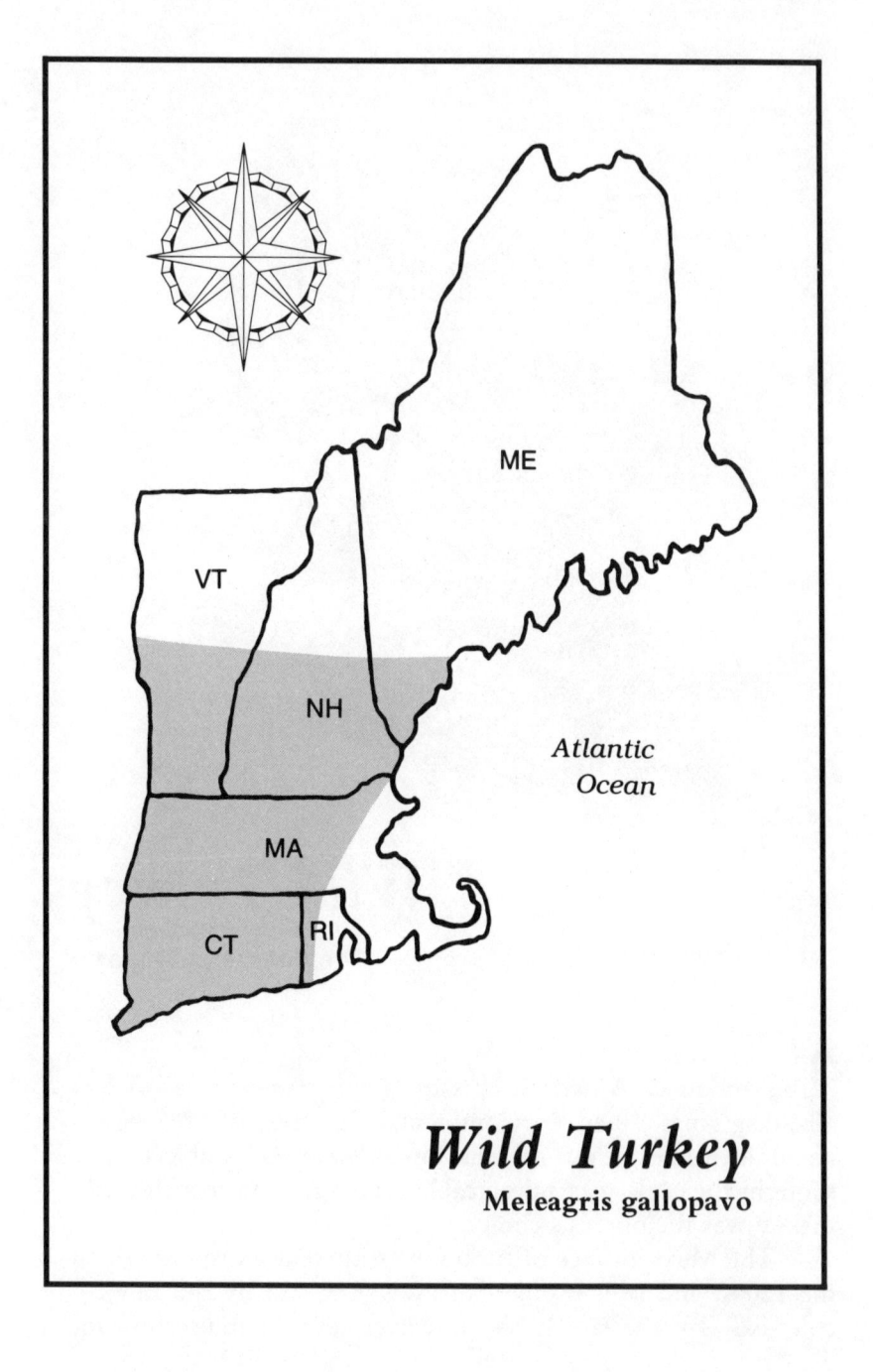

ME

VT

NH

Atlantic
Ocean

MA

CT

RI

Wild Turkey
Meleagris gallopavo

hunting by Pilgrims and Indians, turkeys became scarce. Land clearing fires, lumbering, and much later the chestnut blight, reduced Northeastern populations to a frightening level by the first few decades of this century. Only determined wildlife management efforts have restored the wild turkey to acceptable numbers, and it now breeds in every state except Alaska. Turkey hunting is once again very popular, although this time around there are stringent bag limits and short seasons. No one, including hunters, wants to witness another decline—especially a preventable one.

Field Guidelines

Male birds (toms) stand up to four feet tall, while females (hens) reach about three feet. This wild variety is mainly a smarter, streamlined version of the barnyard gobbler, showing a chestnut-tipped tail instead of white. Adults weigh, on the average, 15 to 20 lbs. Toms, and sometimes hens, sport an 8 to 10-inch "beard"—a feathery tassel that hangs from the chest. Toms blurt out their familiar gobbles, hence the name "gobbler," and hens cluck to their offspring to keep them in line or communicate a warning.

Wild turkeys are forest birds, but prefer the more open type to thick woods. Mast-bearing trees (beech, oak, and to a much lesser extent now, chestnuts) are essential for winter survival, as are shrubs that retain fruit: barberry, rose, sumac, grape, hawthorn, and dogwood. Clearings or fields for summer brooding are also vital; young birds need protein from insects like grasshoppers, beetles, crickets, flies and ants. These areas also provide necessary corn, either on leftover cobs or in manure piles.

Ted Walski, a veteran turkey expert with the New Hampshire Fish and Game Department, reported watching turkeys feed in the *New Hampshire Outdoorsman:* "In July of 1975 I had the luxury of staying in a shack back in the hills of Walpole . . . after I had displaced the porcupines. The first thing I saw one morning was a hen turkey and nine poults (pigeon-sized) about 200 feet away in the middle of a hayfield. All had their heads down looking for insects, primarily grasshoppers, as they slowly moved across the field, the young in a swarm. I watched them for about five minutes and then moved slightly to see better. She either heard or saw me; all of a sudden the poults disappeared. At some command that I couldn't hear or see, they squatted down and froze. The hen did the same. I decided to remain standing motionless to see who would give in first. It was a 'Mexican standoff' for half an hour! Then, either on their own or at another command, the poults suddenly rushed to the hen, and she slunk off with them."

Among dead leaves on the ground, turkeys make a mere depression for a nest. 10 to 15 tan eggs spotted with reddish dots are laid in early spring, followed by a 28-day incubation period. Hens are reluctant to leave the nest while incubating, as seen in this 1840 account by the famous John James Audubon: "I once witnessed the hatching of a brood of turkeys, which I watched for the purpose of securing them together with the parent. I concealed myself on the ground within a very few feet, and saw her raise herself, look anxiously upon the eggs, cluck with a sound peculiar to the mother on such occasions, carefully re-move each half-empty shell, and with her bill caress and dry the young birds. Yes, I have seen this, and have left mother and young to better care than mine could have proved, to the care of their Creator and mine."

Turkeys can roam three or four square miles within their home range, roosting high in different trees at night along the way, often over water for extra security. Large, copious drop-pings on the ground beneath such sites betray their presence. An average bird in the wild might live only two or three years, but extremely wily ones can reach their eighth birthday.

Population and Range

The story of the turkey's comeback is a singularly heartening one; few species have repopulated so rapidly, so strongly, due to human assistance. The eastern wild turkey was extirpated in New England by about 1850, the last strongholds being southern Vermont and the Berkshires of western Massachusetts. Small bands managed to survive in New York's Allegheny Mountains, Pennsylvania, and West Virginia, which formed the basic stock for subsequent restorations.

During the winter of 1968-69, Vermont released 17 wild birds that came from New York, and New Hampshire traded fishers with West Virginia at the same time, introducing 26 turkeys. But as most New Englanders vividly remember, the winters of 1969 and 1970 were brutal; extended cold snaps and heavy snowfall (especially the blizzard of February, 1969) spelled doom for the birds. The first New Hampshire transplants vanished and were forgotten, although the Vermont birds multiplied and lived on. Within five years Vermont had a population of approximately 500 turkeys. Meanwhile, Massachusetts had released 37 New York birds in 1972.

New Hampshire tried again to restore its shrunken population in January, 1975, releasing 27 birds in Walpole, near the Connecticut River. This second attempt proved successful, and since then surplus birds from the Walpole nucleus have been live-trapped and transplanted around southern and central sections of the state. New Hampshire currently supports a population of more than a thousand birds, according to the Fish and Game Department. Massachusetts and Connecticut have about 5,000 each, and Vermont beats all with at least 15,000. Maine released some Vermont turkeys beginning in 1977. A small population exists at the southern tip. And Rhode Island now has a few wild turkeys bordering Connecticut. The cooperation between the Northeastern states has been excellent. All concerned have benefited—especially the birds.

Within 50 years (1930-1980), the U.S. turkey population rose from a low of about 20,000 to about two million. Thanks go to the various state game personnel and other wildlife agencies. Habitat management, controlled hunting, and trap-and-transplant techniques have brought back a formerly extirpated species, even to areas not inhabited before. Trapping by field biologists in the past 25 years has been by the waterfowl "cannon net" method, with great success. Workers put out corn, hide the huge nets with grass, leaves, or snow, and wait in the cold for the birds to arrive. At the right moment they hit a plunger which detonates pellet-packed metal rockets to carry the net over the stunned birds. Inevitably some of those captured are maimed, even killed, but the success rate remains high.

Turkeys have been known to turn on humans, especially when protecting young, as Ernie Belleville learned in 1984. When he gave some imitation calls in Lee, New Hampshire, one day, a juvenile bird appeared, so he dispatched it with a shotgun at 60 feet. As he ran in for the kill, another older, larger turkey flew at him, hit his waist, and knocked him backwards. The gobbler then tried to spur him, so he retreated, later finding his stomach black and blue, and his leg scarred. The turkeys involved here were true wild birds—not the "good old Thanksgiving extra-stupid ones," as biologist Ted Walski terms the domesticated variety. "He's hardly related to the wild turkey," he said. "If you pitched him off a roof, he'd fall like a rock all the way to the ground."

• *Journal Notes* •

January 4, 1984. Hancock, N.H.

I learned something new today, while driving on a dirt road. A turkey flew fast and gracefully with slow wingbeats just ahead of my old Volvo. Another bird followed, gliding toward a lower field. I found their four-inch tracks in the recent dusting of snow, which led me a few hundred feet down the road and into the forest. I also collected some droppings, which as I later learned from Ted Walski, came from both sexes: the straight, three-inch ones were from toms; the smaller, lightbulb-shaped droppings were from hens. I can identify certain species by feces, but with turkeys I can now tell which sex *left its white-tipped calling card. Wonders arise every day for the curious naturalist . . . even in the middle of a backwoods road.*

Mourning Dove

Zenaida macroura

The mourning, or wild, dove is aptly named for its hauntingly mournful cooing, connoting death or a lost love. It is our only dove with a pointed, white-edge tail.

In the early 1900s these doves were often mistaken for passenger pigeons, which were then perilously close to extinction. (The last known individual died in the Cincinnati Zoo in 1914.) The premeditated extermination of wild pigeons left a black mark on America, a blot that can never be erased. The birds formerly numbered in the billions—darkening the skies for hours, by several accounts—until men shot, stoned, clubbed, and netted them out of the trees, day and night. The meat was edible, the feathers were pretty, and the birds were unwarily there for the killing. Few people could have guessed in the 1800s that the birds were non-renewable. After all, flocks were reported to be several miles long, and single trees contained dozens of nests. But the slaughter went on, the beech woods fell, and the one or two eggs laid per clutch couldn't keep up with the mass destruction. The end came quickly. Fortunately the mourning dove is alive, increasing, and not over-hunted.

Field Guidelines

This is a slimmer version of the domestic pigeon, a foot long, including a pointed tail edged in white. The head is brown, and the body is a buffy gray with a bluish hue on the wings. Like other members of its family, the mourning dove has a small beak and weak feet. When taking off it makes a high, loud whistling sound with its wings. The familiar cooing is hollow and remote-sounding, tinged with sadness but also ethereal well-being. The pattern is: Cooah . . . coo, coo, coo.

Roadsides, open fields and parks, farms and lawns are preferred habitats for this dove. It is easily drawn to suburban feeding stations, especially if we scatter cracked corn on the ground. Surrounding shrubs and trees offer added protection.

Other favorite foods include the seeds of bristlegrass, wheat, ragweed, pokeweed, knotweed, and crabgrass. Doves consume very little insect matter, and they are decidedly *not* birds of prey, despite what happened in this anecdote from naturalist Paul Crowley of Bennington, New Hampshire: "About 1981, on a spring morning, I happened to be looking out of the kitchen window when I saw a red squirrel (a regular visitor that I named 'White Eyes') making his usual rounds,

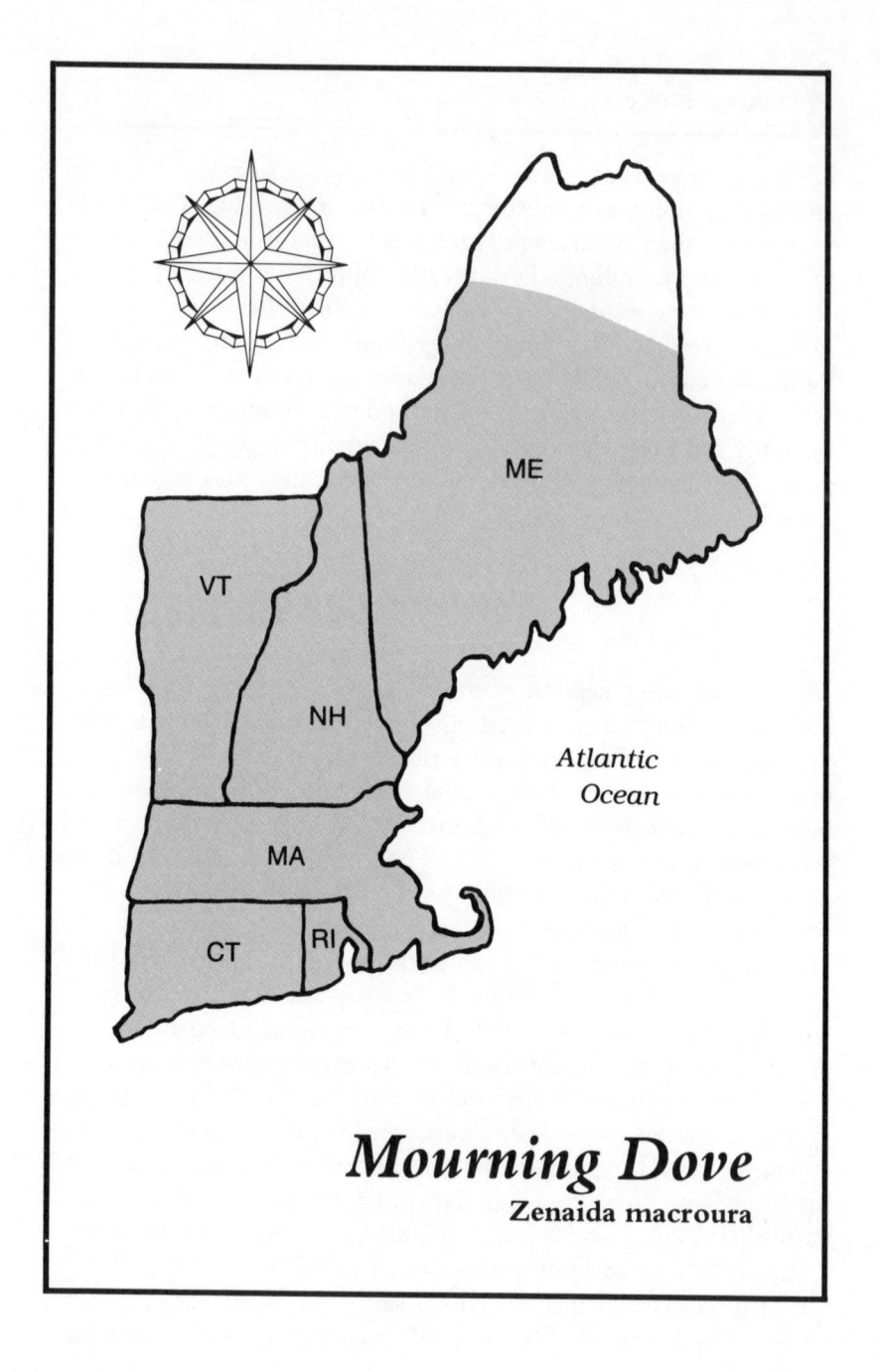

ME

VT

NH

Atlantic
Ocean

MA

CT RI

Mourning Dove
Zenaida macroura

dropping from a hemlock to a beech limb approximately 40 feet above ground. As he ran along the limb, he failed to notice a mourning dove quietly sitting in his path. At the point of near collision he spotted the dove. Suddenly he fell to the ground, running as fast as his little feet would take him into the woods— as if terrified. The dove, unruffled, wondering what happened, cocked his head from side to side with a quizzical expression as if to say, 'Do I look like a hawk?'"

In the South doves nest practically year-round, but in New England April is the usual month to start one of two potential broods. After a week of nest-building, doves lay two white eggs in a shallow platform of sticks, grass, and weeds. Nests are usually placed in conifers 10 to 30 feet from the ground, and the eggs often can be seen from below, through the bottom of the frail nest. It is interesting that several observers have noted that during the 14-day incubation period (as well as later brooding) the male sits on the nest during the day, while the female takes the night shift. The young are well cared for, being fed a regurgitated mix which includes a light-colored liquid from the parents' crop, called "pigeons milk," known for its richness in calcium.

Population and Range

Mourning doves entered the 20th century in good shape, and the past 87 years have seen them expand, especially their winter range. They have benefited from logging and suburbanization, for, although they are rural birds, they also take to residential neighborhoods, including parks, cemeteries, and Christmas tree plantations. Bird-feeding practices, which have increased and improved dramatically since the 1960s, are also responsible for the range expansion.

In Massachusetts, Christmas Bird Counts have shown that the number of doves recorded since 1965 has increased 30 times.

(Because there are now more participants on these counts, however, results must be adjusted accordingly.) New Hampshire
conducts a one-day survey in early February for doves and other
avian invaders, as do other New England states, and the figures
show overwintering doves to be increasing: in 1979, 1,500 were
recorded; in 1980, the figure more than doubled; and by 1985 it
reached 5,600. Frostbite is about the only deterrent keeping
even more doves from wintering in northern New England;
their feet are as delicate as an opossum's ear or tail. Both species
suffer from exposure.

The current breeding range encompasses all of New England except northernmost Maine. Wintering birds inhabit
coastal Maine, most of Vermont and New Hampshire, and all
of the other three states. Wherever seeds are available—whether
at a farm or suburban feeding station—the birds come whistling by.

In the South and West, dove hunting is a very popular
sport, and nationwide mourning doves are harvested more than
all other migratory gamebirds combined. 35 of 48 states now
have seasons, including Rhode Island—the only New England
state. Massachusetts has protected doves since 1903. New
Hampshire, however, came close to opening a season in 1984.
The Granite State's Fish and Game Department proposed *and*
authorized a strict 10-day season, but it was promptly termi-
nated before it began because landowners threatened to post
their property to *all* hunting, thereby denying access. This issue
was an emotional one; hunters wanted another elusive quarry,
while non-hunters considered the dove a songbird, not a gamebird. Inevitably, with continued range expansion and population increases, the species will be hunted legally in more New
England states. This limited shooting of doves will probably
not adversely affect the overall population, but the nagging
question remains: is it ethical to kill a bird that's accustomed to
human handouts?

• *Journal Notes* •

November 6, 1979

At Great Meadows National Wildlife Refuge in Concord, Massachusetts, the witch-hazels are flowering bright yellow through the morning mist. Six blue herons, many geese, teal, and coots readied for flights south, and a small flock of doves passed fast and low over the observation tower. I couldn't help feeling a tinge of sadness—not for the departure of the doves, but for the extinction of their relatives, the passenger pigeons. Never again will any species be so numerous. Mourning doves, not as gregarious, cannot take their place. I wish I could have lived 100 years ago to stand under a night roost, and hear branches break under their tremendous weight. Let's face it . . . there can never be too many birds on this earth.

June 2, 1987

While doing some trail work this morning I flushed a bird that weaved away like a woodcock. I looked around and found a dove nest only five feet off the ground, placed on a broken, horizontal gray birch. It was typically flimsy, with loose bark concealing one side. Two nestlings sat within. I'm surprised they built in such an exposed location, but then again not all humans live in houses. There are individuals out there. Birds are wherever you happen to find them.

Turkey Vulture

Cathartes aura

The turkey vulture, or buzzard as it's called in the West, is the only black bird of prey that soars on upturned wings—a shallow V called a dihedral. *Cathartidae,* the name of the American vulture family, is taken from the Greek, meaning cleanser, a reference to the birds' habit of picking carcasses clean to the bone. Because they do a service for us (cleaning up roadsides and farmlands of fetid bodies), and because the birds themselves stink, vultures have not been persecuted like most raptors. Few are shot or even studied. A person has to have a weak nose and a strong stomach to approach their rank nesting sites, especially those located in caves. They regurgitate on intruders.

Turkey vultures are actually welcomed as avian celebrities each year in Hinckley, Ohio, a town of 2,000 people and about 75 buzzards. The Chamber of Commerce adopted the bird as the town symbol, and on "Buzzard Day," the first Sunday after the Ides of March, some 30,000 onlookers go to the ancestral ledges outside town to gawk at the incoming birds. Honoring such a smelly, hideous-looking bird is heartening. As members of nature's sanitation squad which checks the spread of disease, vultures are guaranteed a relatively hassle-free existence.

Field Guidelines

These are birds of the air, commonly seen drifting over open land, hills, and highways. In flight they are identified by two-toned black wings that span six feet, and by the way these wings angle slightly upward. Vultures often tilt and tip from side to side, adjusting to ever-changing air currents without flapping. At close range they show a red, turkey-like head and exceedingly large nostrils. The bare head is ugly yet functional; it allows the birds to poke inside carcasses without attracting too many parasites that would otherwise cling to feathers.

Turkey vultures are usually silent. Only birds feeding in groups or those disturbed at nests emit high hisses and snarls that match their nasty looks.

Favored meals are soft, ripe carrion. Barnyard animals' feces are also tasted, but only as a side dish. Vultures usually shun living creatures, as they are too much work; their weak talons and beaks make them ill-equipped for killing prey like most raptors. Vultures are adapted to the unsung role of scavengers, recyclers of roadkills, watchers of the dead. Someone has to do it.

Feeding proceeds this way: a bird will clumsily flop to the ground, waddle up to a decaying body, and aim for the eyeballs.

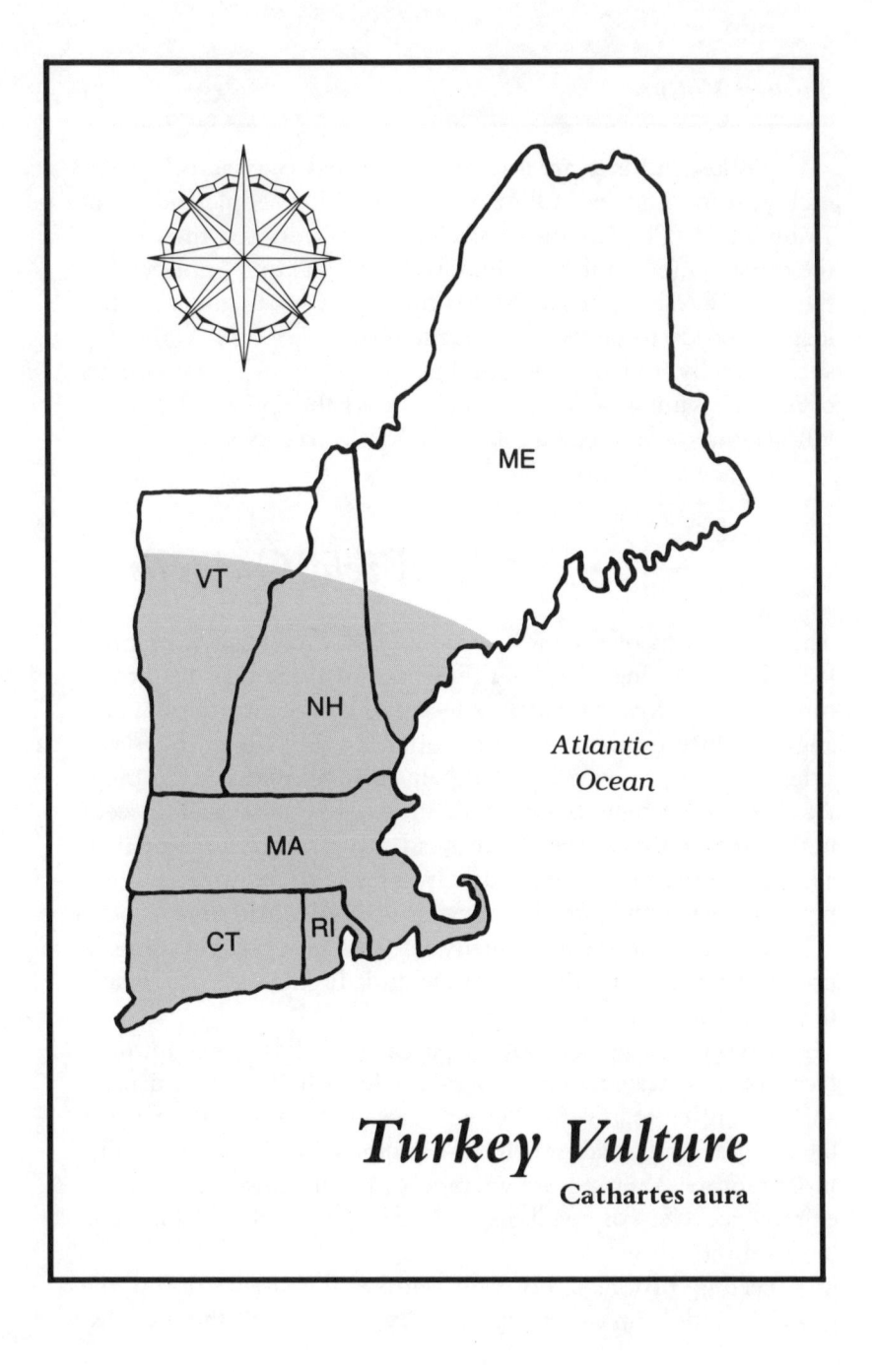

ME

VT

NH

MA

CT

RI

Atlantic
Ocean

Turkey Vulture
Cathartes aura

Then it rips off the skin and eats the muscle and everything else edible. Nothing remains except bones for rodents to finish off. Fully gorged, the bird struggles to rise, leaning forward and tottering along until it hits an updraft, then lifts off as if pulled by puppet strings.

Recent tests have proven that turkey vultures can detect food by smell if the carrion stinks enough. Even simulated gases of decomposition have attracted them when no meat was visible. Besides smelling or seeing the food itself, it is believed that insects also aid them in locating a meal; carrion beetles, which can find dead bodies within minutes, might be *heard* by vultures as the insects scuttle about putrid flesh.

Most nests are on remote, inaccessible cliffs, or in caves or stumps, but a few are placed right on the ground, as Thomas Jackson wrote in Arthur Cleveland Bent's *Life Histories of North American Birds of Prey:* "I found a pair that had taken possession of an abandoned pig-sty in the woods, which furnished them with an admirable place to set up housekeeping. Unfortunately, the smooth board floor had allowed one of their two eggs to roll away, and only one was hatched. Here they were safe from the attack of foxes, raccoons, or other night prowlers."

John Kulish, a veteran trapper, guide, teacher and naturalist from Hancock, New Hampshire, tells of a more traditional nesting site in a neighboring town. "In early spring of 1981 with a little snow on the ground, I was leading a hike over a mountain in Antrim. We came to a rocky dropoff, and I leaned over to check the ledges for bobcat sign. Twenty feet away, two vultures came out of the boulders, and took off right up, higher and higher. They'd heard me coming. There was a lot of whitewash and a few small feathers.

"Vultures were the last thing I expected up there. It was the only confirmed nest in the state that year. In about 1950, I saw one of these birds, which was even more unusual; they were rare up here then. I think they're more beneficial then detrimental. They have their place."

The birds conceal their nests well because the rancid carrion smell attracts predators, especially when adults are feeding the young by regurgitation. Two blotched creamy eggs are laid on a simple base of wood chips, sawdust, or gravel in early spring, and incubated by both sexes. The nestlings' eyes open immediately, and the downy, black-faced chicks move about, hissing, within a week. Two months later the young fledge and join their elders at nighttime roosts. There, shortly before sunset, they drop from the sky to tall, dead trees or buildings with warm chimneys. They ruffle up, preen, and settle to sleep. Not until an hour or so before sunrise do they stir—considerably later than most birds. Ground fog has to clear first, wings must dry, and sun-affected thermals (which enable effortless soaring by the hour) take time to develop. Helios rules the vultures' world.

Population and Range

Until about 1960, turkey vultures were symbols of the South, breeding only as far north as New Jersey, but soon thereafter they silently invaded southern New England, and have steadily spread northward ever since. By the late 1970s some of these black migrants were wintering in the southwest corner of Connecticut, and by 1983 they became more established as breeders in northern New England, summering as far north as Turner and Camden, Maine.

Contributing factors helping to explain this spread include the moderation of climate, an increase in the deer population, hence more available food; and the continued construction of highways, resulting in more roadkills. But it could be something even more basic, such as the passing of time. These are magnificent soaring birds, masters of energy conservation. Thirty miles is just a series of circles and sails to them. It is inevitable, then, that vultures—like ravens—take over wild, craggy mountaintops of new regions. They will keep pushing toward Katahdin, and if the climate continues to ameliorate, they'll scale it by the end of this century. Wherever there's ample death, there'll be plenty of life.

• *Journal Notes* •

August 23, 1982

Folklore has it that wearing a vulture head around one's neck relieves a headache. I don't have a headache, but vultures are on my mind: today I counted 16 of them soaring together over the Sylvania plant in Hillsboro, N.H. These raptors, ugly up close but beautiful on the wing, hang out at the town dump. Despite the fact that they're moving up this way, their image still reminds me of hot, dry days spent on the desert in 1976. I'll look at them as New England residents some year, but for now, their wrinkled, scarlet heads connote the red sandstone country of Arizona.

Eastern Phoebe

Sayornis phoebe

Thomas Say, a 19th-century naturalist from Philadelphia, is honored by the generic name of the phoebe, meaning "Say's bird." It is the sole member of the flycatcher family in New England that pumps its tail up and down.

This winsome, unwary species has the distinction of being the first bird known to be banded. In 1803 John James Audubon studied young phoebes in a cave near Philadelphia, later writing, "When they were about to leave the nest, I fixed a light silver thread to the leg of each, loose enough not to hurt the part, but so fastened that no exertions of theirs could remove it. At the season when the pewee returns to Pennsylvania . . . I found several nests at some distance up the creek, particularly under a bridge, and several others in the adjoining meadows, attached to the inner part of sheds. Having caught several of these birds on the nest, I had the pleasure of finding that two of them had the little ring on the leg."

These are some of the tamest wild birds, as seen in this close encounter by H.H. Brimley in Bent's *Life Histories* series: "I was in a standing position with my rifle under my arm, and I had my hands clasped in front. A faint fluttering of wings caused me to look down, and I saw a phoebe trying to alight on my rifle barrel. Failing to secure a firm grip on the metal, the bird slid down the barrel until the front sight was reached, where it secured the grip desired, and there it perched.

"It showed no sign of fear or nervousness, and in a few seconds flew up and picked a mosquito off my hands. Then, it picked others off the front of my coat, off my sleeves, and several more off my hands. In picking mosquitoes off my face, the sharp points of the bird's bill were noticeably felt at every capture . . . and when I decided to end the incident, I found difficulty in doing so. He continued to perch on my head even after I had started to move around. But my face was beginning to feel somewhat inflamed from the frequent pecking, so I called it a day, and told the phoebe to stop pestering me." (Mr. Brimley wasn't alone; phoebes have also been seen "pestering" deer.)

Field Guidelines

The eastern phoebe is a seven-inch, dull gray bird with a beige breast and a black bill. It is best identified—often at close range—by its repetitious tail-bobbing and by its equally repetitious song, which sounds like its name, accent first syllable. (These rough, emphatic songs are quite different in tone from the soft whistles of *Fee-be,* made by chickadees.) Phoebes also chip sharply in alarm.

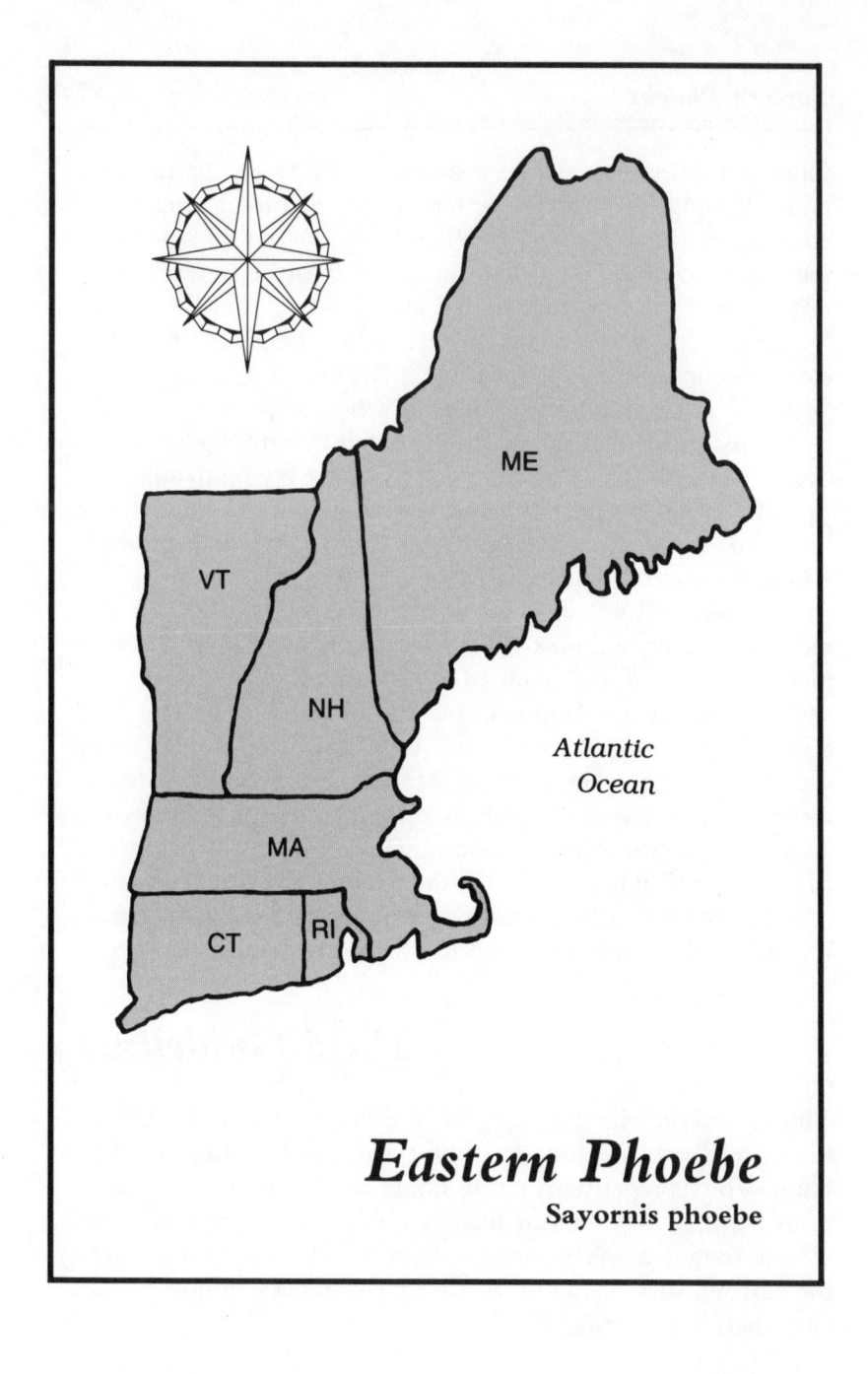

ME

VT

NH

Atlantic
Ocean

MA

CT RI

Eastern Phoebe

Sayornis phoebe

Birdwatchers don't have to venture far from home to find these flycatchers; they live with us, inhabiting towns, farmland, roadsides, and any building with ledges. Besides mosquitoes, they dart from low perches to snatch up bees, flies, beetles, crickets, and grasshoppers—with audible clicks of the beak—then back to the same perch. In early spring and again in the fall, when insects are scarce, phoebes take to fruits of sumac, holly, bayberry, blueberry, and poison-ivy. Most individuals trying to winter in southern New England, however, don't survive on this diet.

When phoebes arrive here they usually encounter receding snow, and ice on the ponds, as mourning cloak butterflies flit around the maple sap buckets of early spring. Soon the birds pair up and start nest-building. For the next week or more the female (mostly) carries mud, grass, and fibers for the base, covers the outside with moss, and lines the inside with hair or fine grasses. New nests are dark, heavy, and wet but soon blend into the surroundings. It is interesting to note, however, that phoebes have adapted imperfectly to civilization; formerly the nests were well camouflaged in caves and on cliffs, but now, on a red barn, for example, the olive-colored nests really stand out.

Phoebes invariably choose sites on shelflike projections, including rafters, windows, girders under trestles and bridges, and over doorways. When backed up to a wall, nests are semicircular, but when placed on a flat surface without siding, they're circular and contain less mud because under such conditions it's not needed as much for adhesion.

The birds seem to like sites that are busy with human activity, nesting only six to eight feet high in places where we can easily reach into the nests. Henry Baldwin, a retired forester from Hillsboro, New Hampshire, writes: "Our present relation with the phoebe is mostly a contest of who will succeed in preventing the birds from nesting on outdoor lighting fixtures and gutters. A few years ago, the phoebes' actions took a more serious turn. Our neighbors in Deering had a camp next to ours, and were entertaining some guests. Several sleepless nights were ascribed to lice issuing from a nearby phoebe nest, and just about caused the evacuation of the camp. No amount of spray-ing—covering myself with repellent, head nets, etc.—did any good. I was obliged to change my sleeping place." To the con-sternation of some people (but to the delight of many others), phoebes use the same nest year after year, although for second broods in the same season, they often build a new one to escape parasites. Anyone wanting to attract these flycatching sprites need only nail up a horizontal board or bracket on a corner of a house or outbuilding—preferably one with an overhang for rain protection.

Around late April in southern New England, and through May in northern sections, phoebes lay three to six white eggs, occasionally spotted. After 15 days of incubation, helpless chicks hatch into a world of cars, farm equipment, and door-slamming, for their habitat is a human one. The nestlings fledge within three weeks, and for the parents it's on to the next brood.

Population and Range

Before white settlers arrived, phoebes nested in rocky ravines and caves—as some of them still do today. There were no outhouses, barns, or bridges. Available nesting sites were prob-ably at a premium. With the steady construction of houses, however, the birds adapted to this new shelter, open land, and the flying insects that hound our pets, farm animals, and our-selves. We tend to develop land near water, which is a plus for phoebes; they're accustomed to aquatic environments, and love to bathe, diving chest-first into any pond.

Their disposition has also aided their spread, for not only are they tolerant of us, they're trusting, and seem to feel com-fortable in our midst. Some still nest ancestrally on remote, rocky ledges, but most now reside with us or in our former dwellings. Almost every deserted shack in the woods harbors a phoebe family.

Phoebes summer across all of New England, and winter south of New Jersey. They are our neighbors for a longer season than most migrants: March through October, depending on latitude. Despite the manner and speed in which we alter the landscape (from natural to artificial), or indeed *because* of it, the phoebes' future looks rosy. The only cloud is habitat loss on Mexican wintering grounds, where the birds spend half the year. Continued destruction of wetlands and savannahs will eliminate many of New England's migrants, especially the already-declining whip-poor-will. Phoebes, at least, are still common enough to spot whenever you open the back door.

• *Journal Notes* •

April 29, 1981

While I was peering at a phoebe nest through an open window of a tumbledown house in the woods, one of the birds flew under my arms and by my binoculars. She landed on the nest (attached to a dangling piece of pressboard from the ceiling), carrying wet grass in her beak. I was startled, but she was calm—one-track-minded on home repairs.

May 14, 1983

Bruce Hedin and I went to the old reservoir today, and as we approached the defunct brick pumphouse, I said, "Great place for phoebes, eh?" He agreed, and seconds later, we found their nest inside with four eggs—atop a wooden post, plunk in the middle of the water. I've always somewhat believed in self-fulfilling prophecies and wishful thinking. Even more now.

April 23, 1985

I found my first real ancestral phoebe nest today. (Two others in remote sites come close, but are nonetheless man-made: inside granite quarries.) It's on the east side of a mountain, attached to the entrance to a rock shelter, four feet high. The mud was still moist. Antisocial phoebes are hard to find these days. I'm glad a few still stick to the old ways.

Tree Swallow

Iridoprocne bicolor

This widespread, familiar swallow is the only species with an all-white chest.

Swallows are birds of the air, gracefully snatching flying insects, and this early migrant sometimes freezes or starves to death due to late snowstorms. Birdwatchers have greatly helped its population and spread by erecting boxes, to the extent that the "tree" of tree swallow is now a kind of misnomer; these birds are more likely seen near man-made nesting boxes than natural tree cavities. Compared with the more specialized barn swallows, the flexible tree swallows—which *can* still nest away from human habitations—stand a better chance of surviving

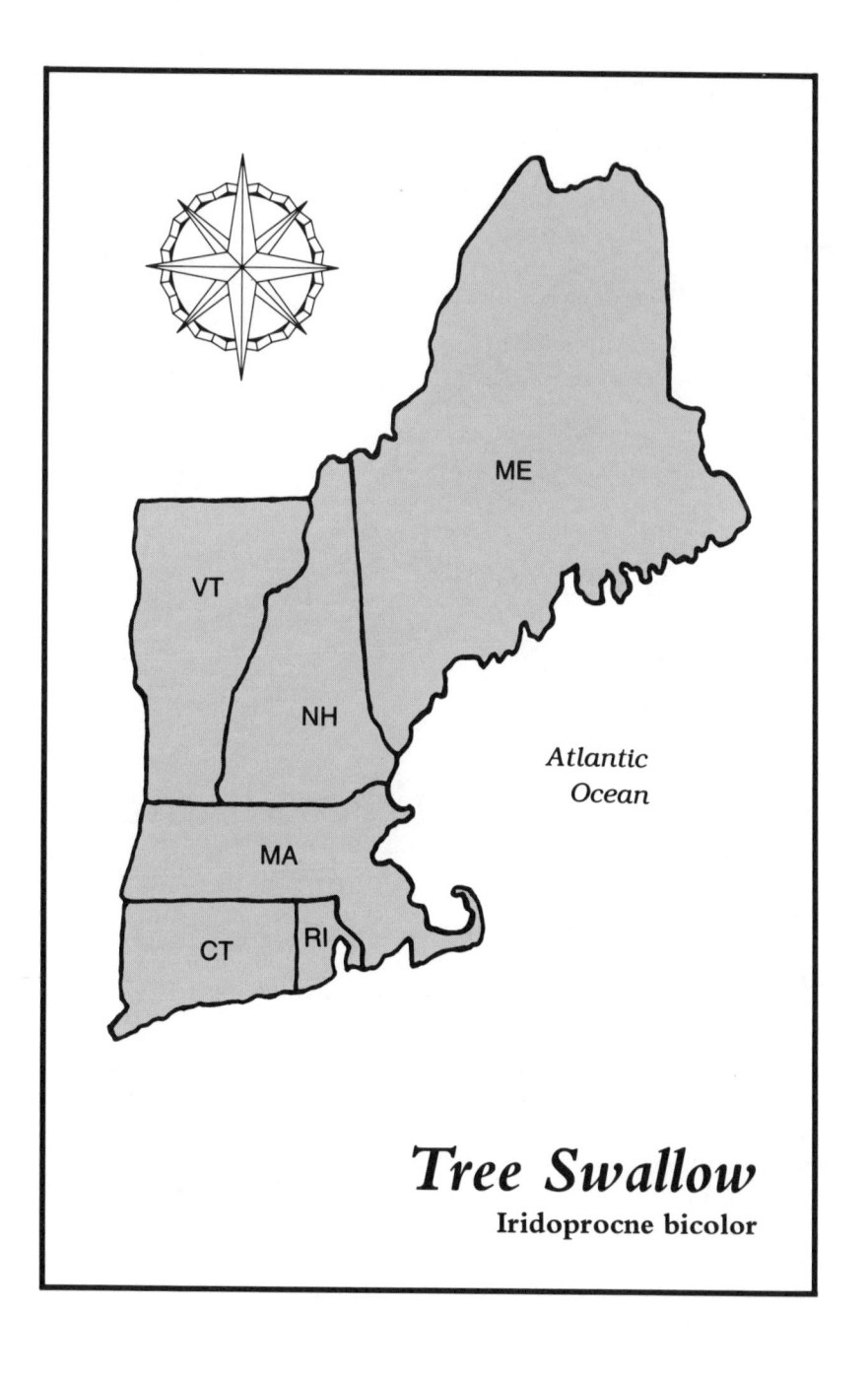

ME

VT

NH

*Atlantic
Ocean*

MA

CT RI

Tree Swallow

Iridoprocne bicolor

through the next century or two. But we must continue to clean out and put up the old birdboxes each April, or the population will shrink.

Field Guidelines

Tree swallows are shiny blue-green above, and white below, with slightly notched tails. Immature birds are dull brown, but still show a white breast. Females attain adult plumage later than males—in their second or third year.

Spring songs by males are liquid warbles and twitters, and, near nests, both sexes give sharp chee-dee notes as they strafe within a few feet of any intruder.

Look for these birds in beaver ponds, marshes, meadows, and open country in general. There they sail high and skim low over water for insects such as flies, bees, beetles, spiders, and ants. On the autumn coast, swallows gorge on the little fruits of the northern bayberry. At New York's Kennedy International Airport in the 1960s, bayberry bushes were planted to hold the soil at runway ends. The result was predictable: tree swallows congregated there by the hundreds whenever bad weather reduced insect activity, and also during fall migration. (The airport is right on the birds' flyway.)

Courtship begins in April or May, involves billing, singing, and mating, and lasts a couple of weeks until incubation starts. Nest-building is an on-and-off process that takes a few weeks; the birds seem easily side-tracked by any distraction, never taking the work very seriously. If nests aren't placed in dead tree cavities, the birds find boxes to their liking: 5 to 10 feet high with entrance holes of one and a half inches. The boxes should be attached to a pole in an open area, and face south for sunlight. Birds also build nests inside fence-posts and mail-boxes, constructing them of grasses and several feathers. Some intrepid pairs have nested on a working St. Lawrence River ferry. They prefer white feathers for lining; on Cape Cod, nearly all nests contain gull feathers.

Three to six white eggs are laid in May or early June in New England, incubated by the female for about two weeks. The nestling stage spans three weeks, and then the young are ready to fly, never to return home. Upon fledging adults and juveniles band together in August at swamps, ocean beaches, and on wires, readying for migration. They make a stunning sight: thousands of swallows perched side by side on telephone lines. At night, they roost communally, rise and form columns in the air, and head south again. Most individuals have vacated New England by the time acorns drop.

Tree swallows act meek on some occasions, yet aggressive on others, as seen by the following accounts sent by Raymond Sprague of Hillsboro, New Hampshire. "Anyone who maintains nesting boxes," he wrote, "is aware of the competition between bluebirds and tree swallows. In general, the bluebirds withstand the constant badgering by the swallows very well, although I have seen and heard of bluebirds being driven away. One time at the farm, however, I observed a different kind of performance. We hadn't seen bluebirds that year, and the boxes were all occupied by tree swallows. About the time the swallows were brooding, a male bluebird appeared. He went from box to box, oblivious to the swallows, and systematically destroyed every nest, throwing the eggs to the ground. This done, he disappeared and we never saw him again.

"While farming, it was my policy to shoot any English sparrows I spotted around my nesting boxes or feeders, so when I noticed a sparrow making a nuisance of himself around a pair of nesting tree swallows, I went for the gun. As soon as the sparrow saw me, he took off—with the swallows in pursuit. They hadn't gone a hundred yards before the swallows drove the sparrow to the ground. One got on his back and held him there—flattened to the ground—and when I came up was busily banging the sparrow on the head. I stood within three feet of him, and it was obvious that he wasn't making much impression with his soft, flycatcher beak, although the sparrow didn't seem too happy about the whole affair. I don't know how long he might have continued, but when he became aware of me standing over him, he flew off and left me to polish off the sparrow—which I did."

Population and Range

The natural reforestation which has engulfed much of New England during the past 50 years hasn't totally hindered these open-country birds because, coupled with the beaver's comeback, swallows gain prime nesting sites in shallow beaver ponds that feature drowned trees. The implementation of innumerable birdhouses has also upped swallow numbers, as has *de*forestation in Central America. Tropical forests about the size of Maine are being clearcut each year for cattle grazing/beef exportation. Open land means better habitat for wintering swallows, buntings, etc., although not for nighthawks or whip-poor-wills. Tourism, money madness, and an expanding population in Central and South America might uproot many of our migrant songbirds, but perhaps not swallows; they stand to benefit from fast food hamburger profits.

Tree swallows are common summer residents across New England. All we have to do to increase their population (thereby reducing the insect pest population), is make simple wooden boxes for them. Iridescent beauty veering by in the sunlight is cheaply bought.

• *Journal Notes* •

May 17, 1982

Observed an adult tree swallow (male?) on the ground, pecking at a second-year female's eye, holding her down. I stood over them in the grass as they parted. The female then dove into a nesting box, pursued by her aggressor. After ten minutes of noisy flapping and squawking, he left and she followed. More abuse? At first I had thought they were fighting, but then realized it was just the usual resist-accept ritual. The mating game, pleasurable in the end, can surely start off violently.

May 14, 1982

A pith helmet might have come in handy! As I approached a backyard swallow box, one bird struggled out of the hole, while another came charging from the side. Both of them repeatedly divebombed me within three feet of my head, emitting short series of gurgling notes similar to the beginning of a marsh wren's song. I took the hint and slunk away to check on other less aggressive box-nesters.

Chimney Swift

Chaetura pelagica

Swifts are sleek, fleet, insect-eating birds, almost always airborne. They rarely perch, being capable of drinking, bathing, and possibly even copulating in flight, and have been known to fly 80 miles a day while migrating. Surely they cover that distance almost daily, just weaving back and forth across the sky. Nests of some species of Old World swifts (made of the birds' saliva) comprise the Asian delicacy popularly called bird's-nest soup.

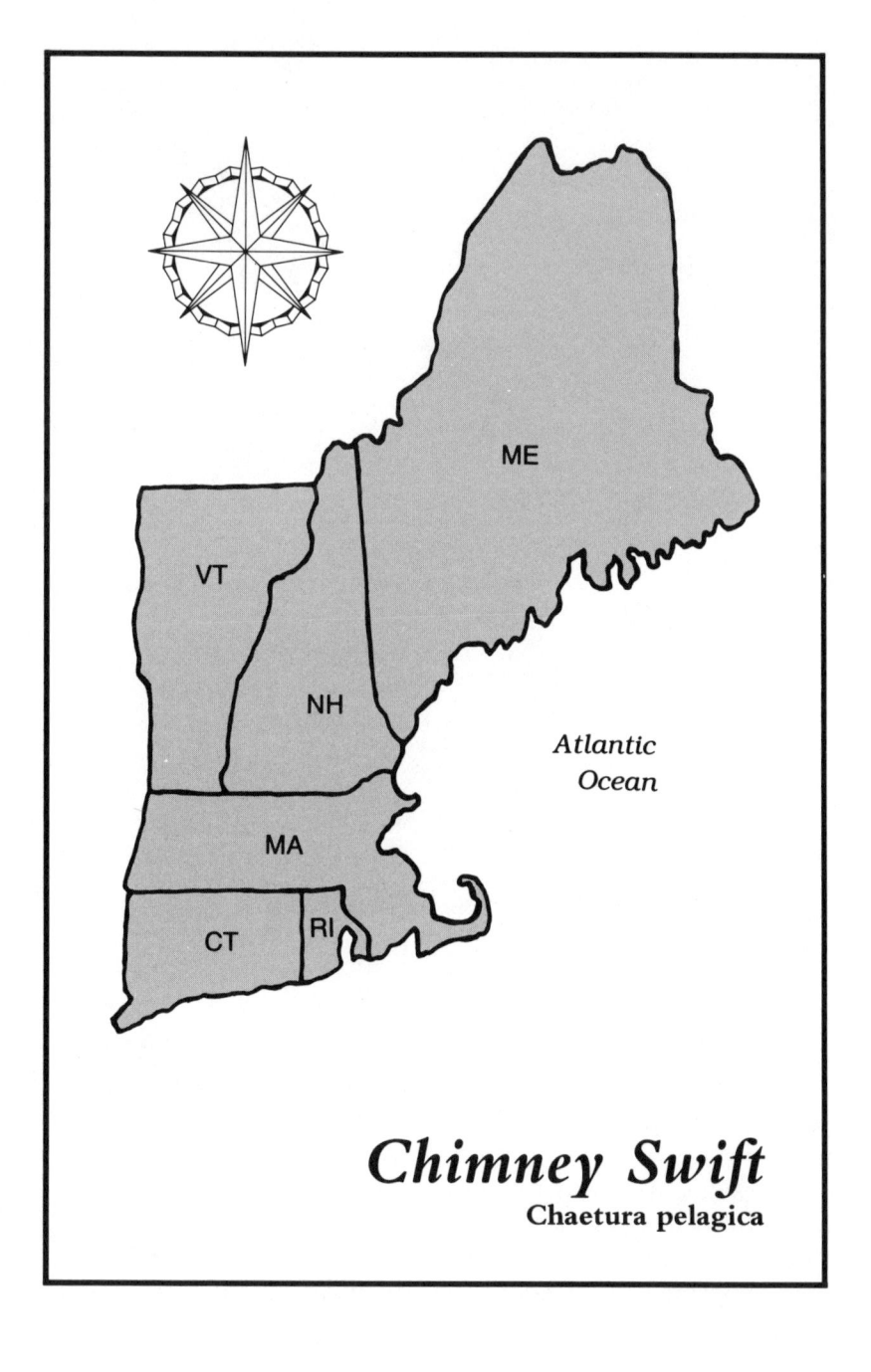

ME

VT

NH

Atlantic
Ocean

MA

CT RI

Chimney Swift
Chaetura pelagica

The chimney swift is the only genus of the species in the East. Its wintering grounds were unknown until 1944. Much remains to be learned about these "flying cigars" who furtively nest and roost in our homes.

Field Guidelines

Five-inch, charcoal birds with long, pointed wings, swifts appear to be tailless and footless. (Actually, the short, stiff tail is rarely spread, and the feet are weak and small, hence the family name of *Apodidae;* without feet.) Unlike the low, smooth skimming of swallows, the swifts' high flight is more batlike— erratic fluttering and gliding in circles. For some inexplicable reason, the birds often fly in groups of three, twittering loudly in rapid, mechanical tones.

People tend to look down or straight ahead as they walk; to see chimney swifts, look up . . . way up. They are commonly spotted over towns and cities near where they breed. During spring and fall migrations, swifts congregate in huge numbers at communal roosting sites, as described by teacher-naturalist Mike Zettek: "On a warm June evening in Brattleboro, Vermont, I joined two friends for a movie at a downtown theatre. It was still twilight when the movie finished, and as we exited, people were stopped on the sidewalk with heads craned skyward. I sensed my eyes and ears go into overdrive, for the spectacle was the low circling of thousands upon thousands of . . . ? As we gazed, I elbowed my friends in amusement at some of the comments we overheard: 'Must be bats,' 'I think they are swallows.' A jokester looked at his girlfriend and chided, 'I *do* believe in spooks, I do, I do, I do!'

"From the circling swarm, a funnel formed and joined the top of a tall brick smokestack. Looking closely, I made out individual birds spiralling down, and dropping right into the stack. Wanting to get a better view, we dashed up creaky stairs of an old apartment building, popped open a window, and climbed onto the roof—six stories up. Less than half of these 'flying cigars' were still airborne, but what a sight. Against the afterglow of a splendid sunset, we'd witnessed perhaps more than 5,000 swifts getting swallowed up by an obsolete smokestack that seemed like a magical vacuum, cleaning the air rather than polluting it. As we watched the last swift drop out of sight, we hoped out loud that this was a promising vision of a post-industrial world."

Roosting swifts bunch up like bats, but cling head up, not down. Nesting, however, is done singly, one pair per chimney. Upon arrival in New England in May, pairs gather short sticks less than two inches long while flying, grabbing with the feet, and transferring to the bill en route back to the nest. The sticks are cemented together with glutinous saliva that the birds produce and attached to a vertical wall, usually at least 10 feet down from the chimney top. The semi-circular cups are also glued to old wells, barns, silos, and inside air shafts. Rarely are caves or hollow trees used anymore.

Four or five white eggs are laid in June, incubated by both sexes. About two weeks after hatching the young fledge, but remain close to the nest for another fortnight. Rain and the use of fireplaces during summer cool spells cause many lost nests and burnt chicks.

Dave McMurray, a farmer from Hartsville, Tennessee, and environmental engineer with the Occupational Safety and Health Administration in Nashville, witnessed dead swifts aplenty in April, 1975. "We got a call at the State Health Department about kids blacking out in a Lebanon grade school, about 30 miles away. We told them to evacuate immediately: sounded like carbon monoxide (CO). A National Guard helicopter landed us in the schoolyard half an hour later. There was CO throughout the school, and many kids were already at the hospital. Gas-fired furnace? Yep. They had just fired it back up after a three-week warm spell.

"We opened up the cleanout door at the bottom of the chimney, and . . . Lordy, Lordy! There were literally hundreds of birds—dead swifts—blocking the flue. Evidently they had settled in during the warm spell and had a little chimney swift Hilton going for them. Then the furnace had been fired for the cold snap, and it was carbon monoxide—colorless, odorless, silent quick death for the occupants. The exhaust gases, having nowhere to go through the blocked chimney (we estimated 500-1,000 dead swifts), dumped into the school and asphyxiated the kids. (None died.) I recommended special screens for the tops of the chimneys, and I get to see them every time I drive to Nashville."

Mr. McMurray also wrote of a face-to-face encounter with a *live* swift: "We came home to Hartsville one night, got halfway through the livingroom, and then hit the floor as I was being attacked by something in the room making a loud sound. It scared the hell out of me, and I am rather melodramatic. The light was switched on, and I saw this thing hanging on the wall about a foot from the ceiling. It was a chimney swift with no sense: first he went out the wrong end of the chimney; secondly, I opened the front door wide, shut the livingroom off, and got the bird flying around, and it actually clung to the wall *above* the doorway.

"After an hour of exciting futility, the cat wandered in and divined the situation in an instant, catching the bird and heading out the door. We covered the fireplace opening, but still have little white spots on the walls as reminders. They come about every year, and raise a family. They're welcome, at least in our chimney."

Population and Range

The chimney swift is one of the few bird species that has bene-fited from modern civilization's home-building activities. There's no telling how it would have fared without the spread of people and their homes, but today there are more nesting sites available and thus a few more swifts. From May through Labor Day swifts are a common sight overhead, although they are solitary, localized nesters. They'll be in and around our homes as long as chimneys remain standard fixtures, providing not too many are cleaned during the nesting season. Swifts have adapted to us; now we should be flexible and adapt to them. It's a matter of timing and consideration.

• *Journal Notes* •

May 6, 1984

While watching the first swift of the spring descend into a chimney at dusk, I thought back to the fourth grade when my interest in birds was budding. When a swift entered a high classroom window, I was chosen to identify and catch it, since I already had a reputation as a birdwatcher (and a height advantage over everyone else). I don't remember the particulars, but I managed to trap it against the wall and release it out the door, after we examined it. The incident was discussed at great length that day, and from then on, I was a birdmaniac.

August 12, 1985

A friend and I sat on a mattress atop a ridge, facing the East, a picnic basket by our side. From 11 pm to 2 am, we counted 83 celestial streaks as part of the annual Perseid meteor shower. Most of them emanated from the North, heading southwest. Several times during the watch we heard chimney swifts chirping from the big house behind us. The moon was not up; we wondered why they called out. The night poses many questions to nightowls, and the answers come about once in a blue moon. But we keep on searching.

Northern Raven

Corvus corax

The raven, the only all-black bird with a wedge-shaped tail, has the distinction of being the largest songbird in the world. It is a member of the *Corvidae* family which also includes crows, jays, and magpies—all relatively intelligent birds. Ravens have always carried a reputation for evil and mischief, and Edgar Allen Poe's immortal poem furthered this image when he wrote of "this grim, ungainly, ghastly, gaunt, and ominous bird of yore." Even today ravens cause trouble: in February, 1984, a foul-mouthed pet bird escaped and showed up at a schoolyard in Barker, New York. Students couldn't concentrate on their studies with repeated croakings of, as the media put it, "a common two-word directive."

Field Guidelines

Ravens can be more than two feet long, with a wingspan of four feet, which they use to soar like hawks. At extreme close range (a rarity for birders), shaggy throat feathers show, but the best way to differentiate them from crows is by calls: ravens croak; crows caw. The gutteral croakings are varied, some deep, some high-pitched gurgles. All are wild-sounding, for this is a wilderness bird that has retreated from the civilization that foolishly shot and poisoned them.

Look for these beguiling scavengers around coastal cliffs, mountain forests of the North, and rugged country in general. Along the seashore they rob gulls and terns of their eggs. Elsewhere they feast on insects, berries, live or dead fish, frogs, crayfish, and rodents. Indigestible matter is ejected from the mouth in the form of pellets, similar to those of hawks and owls. These castings are composed of bones, stones, and shells, often wrapped in grass.

Some birds even try spiny carcasses, as reported by Willard Viall: "In 1957, we were driving to Roaring Brook Camp at Baxter Park, when we surprised a northern raven experimenting with a porcupine which had been killed on the little road near Windey Pitch. We stopped instantly and got out for a better look, when, with a gutteral oath, he flew up to a high branch just overhead in a dead tree. He landed on it and then rose up several feet as from a trampoline. This he repeated two or three times with increasing indignation and appropriate remarks apparently addressed to us. His third or fourth landing was done expertly on one foot, and in the raised foot I could see through my glasses that he had picked up a quill, by now well embed-

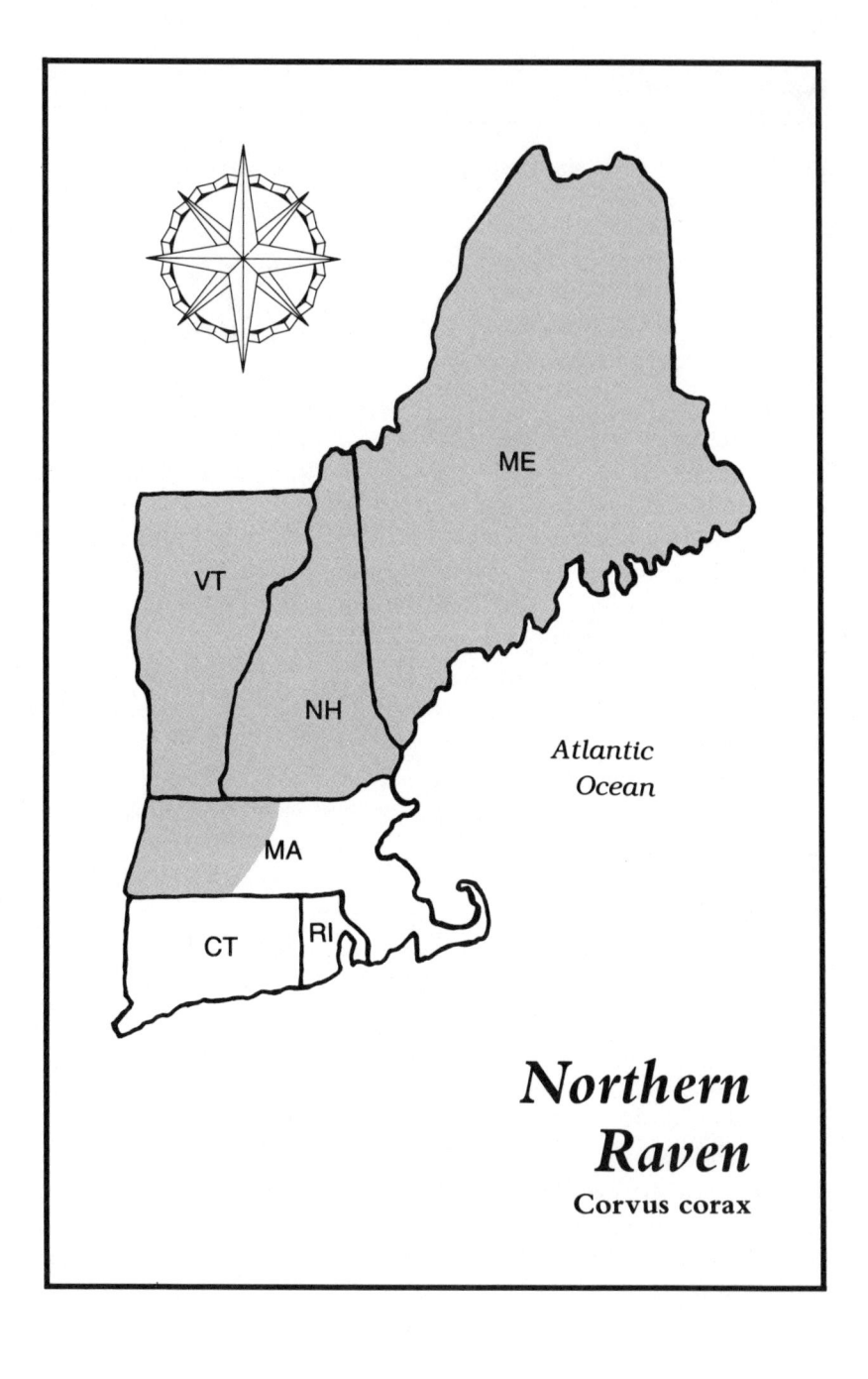

**Northern
Raven**

Corvus corax

ded. This he at once vigorously set about removing, interrupting the painful operation to cock his head, glare down at us, and say emphatically what he thought of us.

"We were tempted to stay to see a successful end to his difficulty, but feared we would drive him off before he accomplished it. Our unsuppressed laughter contributed nothing except volume to his expressions of outrage, so we left him at his work. Several hours later, on return, we were glad to see that the porky had been well dined on, probably by our bird and his friends. I had seen ravens around Mt. Katahdin since my first visit in 1931, but this was the first intimate view of one. Very pleasant for us if not for him."

Ravens are very early breeders, building eyrie-type nests beginning in late February or early March. The work of lugging big sticks takes about two weeks; the end result is a nest two to four feet in diameter, lined with deer or sheep hair, mosses, and grasses. Favored sites are on cliff ledges, or high in a coniferous tree. Some birds, however, take to man-made sites, as Ben Allison reported: "Alstead, our southwestern New Hampshire town, is really on the fringe of the raven's nesting range. However, in our surrounding hills with elevations of 1,300-1,800 feet, we have several abandoned mica and feldspar mines in isolated areas. During the past few years, I have discovered raven nests in three of these mines—all located on small niches high on the mine walls."

Other artificial nesting sites are listed in Bent's *Life Histories* series: "Several different parts of windmills; rafters in small shacks; in barns; in various places in houses; and one on top of a bookcase in a schoolhouse. In the low, river country (of Washington State), where natural sites are scarce, we have found the nests on high-tension poles, oil derricks, telegraph poles, and on the beam of a railroad bridge." (In 1976, at Yellowstone National Park, I found a nest containing four chicks on a beam under a small road bridge. The parents ignored the cars, but squawked boisterously whenever I crossed.)

In northern New England, where most of the raven population lives, females lay four to seven greenish eggs during March or early April, and a three-week incubation period follows. During the month-long nestling phase the young birds befoul the nest rim, backing up to the edge and squirting whitewash over the side. Most of the lime reaches the rocks below, but some paints their home. Whitewashing against dark rocks catches our eyes, and is a reliable clue for finding nests. Also during the nestling phase young birds are obvious by their calling; they sound like someone screaming while being throttled.

Come autumn, and on through winter, ravens move around in small flocks, searching for better feeding areas, but they are largely non-migratory. Paul Roberts, a skilled and dedicated hawkwatcher, wrote about an experience in September, 1982: "I was watching migrating broad-winged hawks from the summit of Mt. Wachusett, Massachusetts. Several small kettles of broadwings had been thermalling up to the Northeast, when suddenly I spied two non-broadwings soaring up over the hills. These birds were longer and slimmer, but the lighting was terrible. They were only minute silhouettes against the distant landscape. The flight was intriguing. The two birds were flying in much wider, looser, lazier circles than did the broadwings. Even using a powerful spotting scope, we could pick up little on these increasingly mysterious figures. Splaying to maximize lift in mediocre soaring conditions, the wings looked like those of a soaring falcon. My first unspoken thought on identification was, however, that these might be Cooper's hawks. Their behavior closely resembled that of the few migrating Cooper's we see from Mt. Wachusett. Slowly, almost aimlessly, the birds drifted closer to the summit, soaring low, beneath our observation site. Then the large head, the distinctive beak, and the long, wedge-shaped tail grew apparent. Ravens! Our first ravens in seven years of hawkwatching on Wachusett! One of the few sightings in the eastern half of the state in many years! For many hawkwatchers there that day, it was a state bird; for some, a life bird. For all, it was something special. Since then ravens have been seen every spring and fall, and there is reason to believe that they are breeding in the vicinity of the mountain."

Population and Range

Since the mid-1950s, ravens have been moving southward from Maine. Although gone from parts of their former range (ousted by civilization), they've been taking over new territories. By the late 1970s they were increasing in southern New Hampshire and Vermont, and in June, 1983, a nesting pair made big news at Quabbin Reservoir in western Massachusetts. Reforestation, which has enveloped much of central and northern New England—especially since the 1940s—could be the main reason.

The current breeding range encompasses most of Maine, hilly, wild regions of Vermont and New Hampshire, and limited sections of western Massachusetts. The species is also expanding its range in the Appalachians. Ravens will undoubtedly be recorded more frequently in New England in future years, due to increasing numbers of birds *and* birdwatchers who don't automatically dismiss them as crows. All big, black birds are "just crows"? Nevermore.

• *Journal Notes* •

March 1, 1983

To some people, keeping a folding chair beside a remote pond would seem a bit soft. They'd be right, of course. But I use that chair under the Paul Bunyan pine, 20 feet from the water, to rest quietly and observe, hoping for wildlife to pass by. It's called still-watching. After awhile you blend into the background, and if the wind is favorable, the creatures don't detect you until they're on top of you. It was 45 degrees this morning, and as I faced the sun, dozing, I was awakened by a calling raven to the East. I didn't mind at all.

April 9, 1983

I fell asleep again in my chair, only to awake to a croaking raven. It soared just like a buteo and even plunged in tear-drop shape, apparently playing.

December 9, 1983

For the third time, a raven awoke me in the pond chair. Groggy, I looked up at the setting sun, wondering how close the raven's nest . . . wondering if they see me . . . wondering about the improbability of me ever waking up a raven from its roost.

May 17, 1984

A day to rave about: Paul Crowley and I, after four hours of concerted effort amid the black flies, found an active raven nest—one of three known in southern New Hampshire. Going up the mountain, we'd seen an adult bird land on a nearby boulder, but somehow we missed the site. Hours later, on the way down, Paul was ahead of me when he spotted a huge pile of sticks on the ground. Then he looked up, saw whitewashing and the nest above, and called me over. The nest is attached to a steep rock wall about 30 feet above a wooded ravine, and contains three half-grown young. Judging by the pile of accumulated sticks from previous nestings—measuring four feet high and six feet across—

we guessed the ravens had used the same site for several years, although not necessarily consecutively. Here, in a popular Audubon sanctuary, the sneaky ravens had avoided detection. Until now.

Tufted Titmouse

Parus bicolor

This is the only small, gray bird sporting a crest. The tufted titmouse is a member of the *Paridae* family, whose British relatives are extraordinarily clever; since World War II, tits have learned from each other to open and drink from doorstep milk bottles. They tear the cardboard caps, and hammer at those made of aluminum foil. Titmice in our country have not shown a taste for milk, but are some of the first birds to locate newly-erected feeders.

Field Guidelines

The tufted titmouse is sparrow-sized, mouse-gray with rusty sides, a white breast, and a prominent crest.

Calls are series of loud, clear whistles that are repeated often and throughout the year. Eliot Taylor can imitate these calls (among many others), and sent this anecdote on his ability: "One spring day in 1965, I was coming out of the woods at Crooked Pond in Boxford, Massachusetts, with the Brookline Bird Club, when I heard a tufty calling about a quarter-mile away. 'Tufted titmouse,' I yelled, and I started whistling its Peter-Peter calls. The bird was coming closer just as a lady asked me to stop whistling because she wanted to hear the bird—not me. I kept on whistling and she kept on asking me to keep quiet as the bird came in closer. After three minutes or so, the titmouse flew across the street and landed on a branch 10 feet above us. I politely told the lady that I would now stop whistling."

The titmouse's realm is moist, deciduous woods, but it also comes to residential areas. In winter, in the company of chickadees and nuthatches, it feeds on oak and beech mast, and visits feeders where sunflower seeds are provided. During warmer months, tomtit eats caterpillars, wasps, ants, and spiders.

Titmice are cavity nesters, building their softly-lined homes inside trees or birdboxes. Like the great crested flycatcher, titmice have the unusual habit of decorating nests with string, cellophane, and especially shed snakeskins. If enough of the right kind of lining is not available, the birds sometimes pluck hair from rodents and pets. Even humans aren't immune to attack, as seen in this 1925 account written by Vitae Kite: "He lit squarely on top of my head, giving me such a start that it was with great difficulty I controlled myself and sat still. My hair has been white for many years, but I still have plenty of it, and was more than willing to divide with this little bird, so I steadied

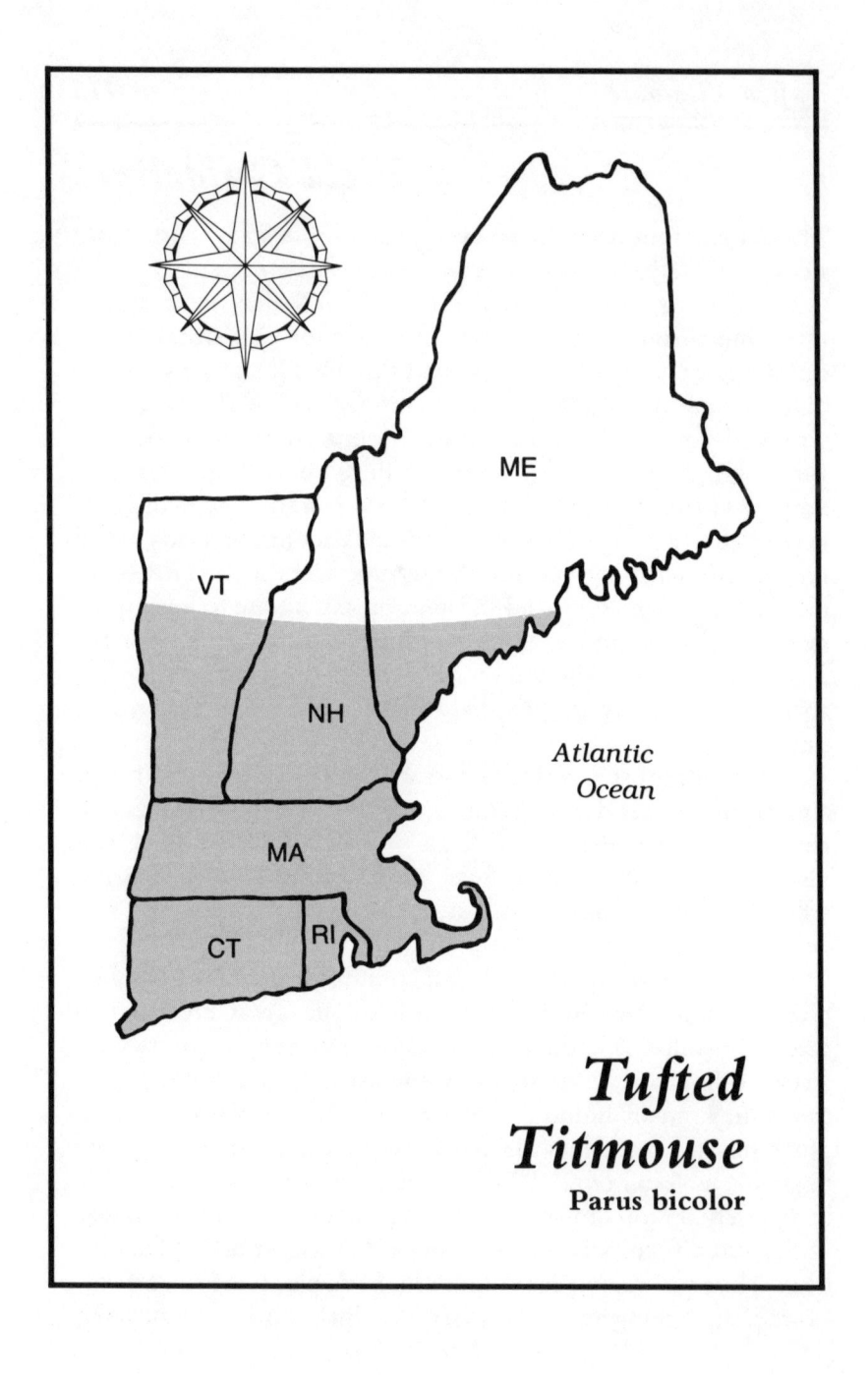

ME

VT

NH

Atlantic
Ocean

MA

CT   RI

Tufted
Titmouse
Parus bicolor

myself while that energetic Tom had the time of his life gathering 'wool' to line his nest."

Irwin Smith once wrote of a similar assault: " . . . the third time it came back, instead of flying away again, it lit on my head, and, in a very diligent manner, began to pick the hairs therefrom. The pricking of its sharp little toes on my scalp, and the vigor of the hair-pulling was a trifle too much for my self-control, and I instinctively moved my head. Away it flew, but only for a moment, and then it was back at work, harder than before."

In April or May females lay five to eight white eggs that are speckled with brown. During the two-week incubation period the female sits tight, even when nosy birders poke around the nesting site, as they are wont to do. Less than three weeks after hatching the young fledge, but only travel in the company of their parents. As wild geese head south over frosty fields, the titmice join kinglets, creepers, and other non-migratory birds. New England's winter woods may be bleak to some, but they're surely not barren or lifeless in reality—not with chickadees and titmice flitting from tree to tree like miniature acrobats, disdaining the severest weather.

Although our titmice do not raid milk bottles as they do in England, they show the intelligence of memory, as proven in this Mabel Gillespie report of 1930: "During one night, there was a fall of very soft snow, with a succeeding drop in temperature. The banding traps were all removed but one, lest they should become frozen in the ice crust. After the freeze, the outline of each trap was clearly visible in the crust. A titmouse flew to the ground at the spot directly in front of the outlined mark of an entrance funnel. This showed that the bird clearly remembered the location of the funnel. Then, however, just as it was about to run forward, it appeared to realize that the trap was not there. The bird hesitated, looked about, and observed that another trap was in its accustomed place. It flew to this trap and entered for food."

Population and Range

Until the early 1950s tufted titmice ranged only as far north as New York and New Jersey. The first known Massachusetts nest was discovered in 1957, and, in the fall of that year, there was an unprecedented influx of thousands of these southern birds to Maine and New Hampshire. No one knows why.

Since then tufties have invaded new territories at a relatively rapid pace, thanks largely to more people feeding the birds in winter. Massachusetts and New Hampshire conduct cardinal/titmouse/mockingbird surveys each February, counting all individuals seen during a two-day period, and the results show a steady increase: in New Hampshire in 1979, observers counted 466 titmice; in 1980, 876; by 1986 the count was over 1,300. Christmas Bird Counts also reflect a northward spread, particularly in coastal Maine.

The current permanent range of the species covers all of Connecticut, Rhode Island, and Massachusetts, in addition to southern Vermont, New Hampshire and Maine. Continued mild winters, along with our habit of feeding wild birds, should help extend the range even more. Some year soon titmice might reach boreal regions of spruce and fir, and, being seen in the company of Yankee chickadees, will be thought of as natives— not southern immigrants.

• *Journal Notes* •

April 2, 1978

While en route to Henry Beston's Outermost House on Cape Cod (or, the remains thereof, following February's blizzard), I heard a titmouse calling above the high sea scarp. Twenty years ago this would have been big news in the birding world; prior to 1955, there were only 15 titmice recorded in all of Massachusetts. Now a sighting on the Lower Cape—or anywhere else in the state—is strictly back page. As has been said and sung, the times truly are a-changing.

Carolina Wren

Thryothorus ludovicianus

This sparrow-sized bird is the largest wren likely to be seen in the East. Its generic name, *Thryothorus,* is from the Greek, meaning reed-leaping—referring to one of its favorite habitats, swamps. The Carolina wren belongs to the family *Troglodytidae,* which is somewhat of a misnomer; only the canyon wren of the West approaches being a true "cave dweller."

Field Guidelines

Reddish brown above and buff below, this wren has a prominent white stripe over the eyes. Like other wrens it jerks its cocked tail when distressed, and is constantly moving and bobbing about.

Both sexes sing (often a duet) loud, three-syllabled phrases all year long—a rarity among birds. Songs vary with the region of the country, even from state to state. Olive Rhines, a veteran birdwatcher from New Hampshire, recalls the singing in her early days in Connecticut: "The male kept up a constant, varied song, sometimes imitating the notes of other species. As the day ended and most birds had retired to their night perches, the wren seemed to wish to prolong the day with one more snatch of music. It seemed no accident that when I walked abroad at dusk (no matter what part of the grounds), the wren would find me, perch close above my head and warble, *sotto voce,* a brief cadenza, so sweet and lyrical as to make me hold my breath in sheer pleasure. He seemed to watch me closely as I listened. Then with a sudden twitching motion he would slip furtively away to the barn and disappear for the night. It was almost as though he was singing 'good night'! This same behavior, with different musical phrases, was repeated throughout two nesting periods. I shall never forget the experience."

Carolina wrens inhabit thickets, ravines, brushpiles, and rural backyards. In such tangles, they hunt ants, bees, millipedes, beetles and weevils, caterpillars, crickets, and spiders. Vegetable matter, which comprises only a small percentage of the diet, includes seeds of bayberry, poison-ivy, sumac, and sweet gum.

Like other wrens, the Carolina sometimes builds a domed nest with a side entrance, but unlike some species, the male does not make "dummy" nests before his mate decides on the final site, which she then lines with feathers, moss, fur, or wool. External parts of nests are made of leaves, twigs, and bark, and

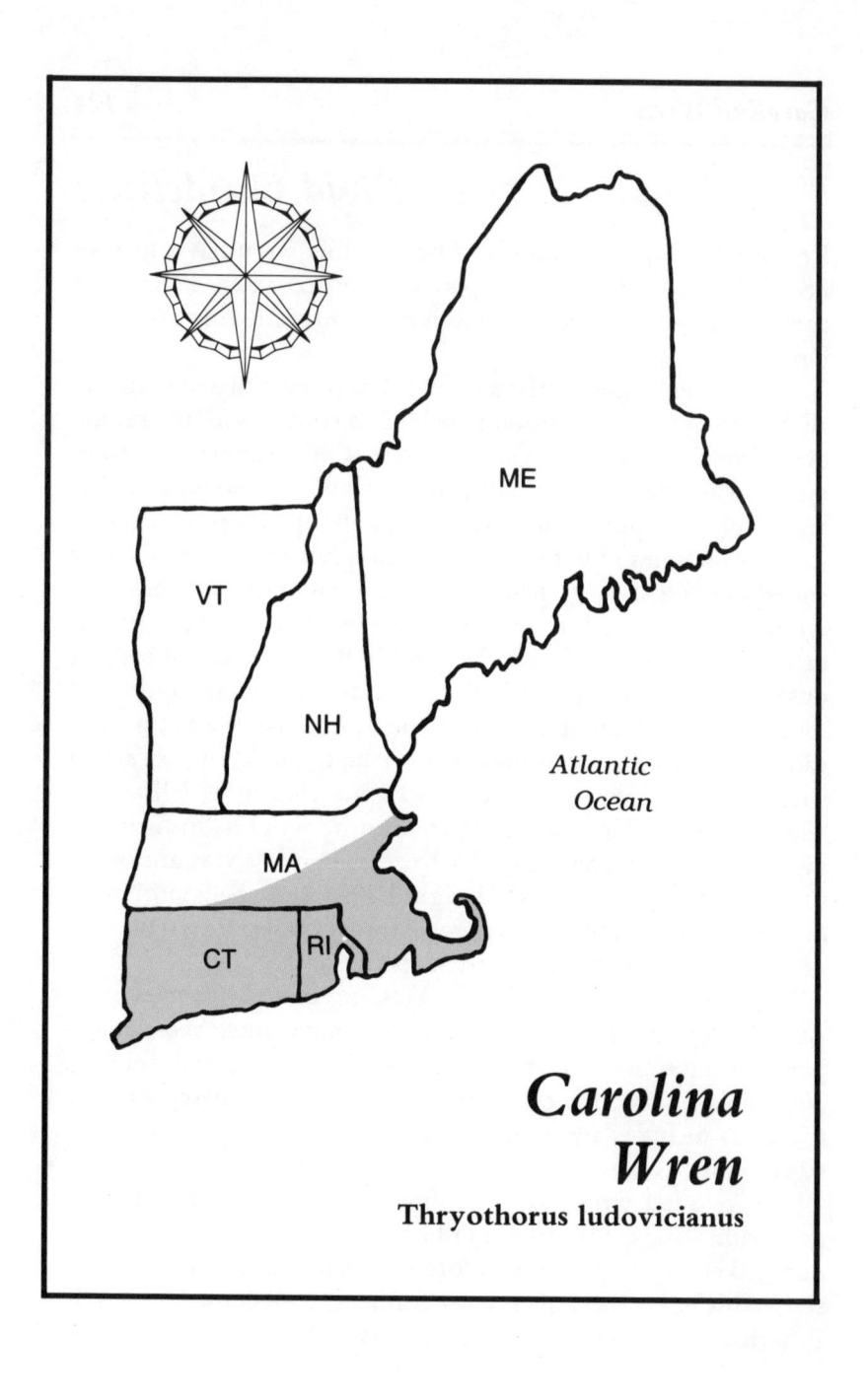

ME

VT

NH

*Atlantic
Ocean*

MA

CT   **RI**

*Carolina
Wren*

Thryothorus ludovicianus

locations vary greatly: inside trees or birdboxes, on stone walls, upturned roots, or attached to buildings. Nests have also been found in discarded cans, pots, hats, mailboxes (some while in use), and pockets of clothes on the line. Marion Boermeester, formerly of Needham, Massachusetts, learned of this species' ways at her current home in North Carolina in 1984: "A pair nested in my newly-purchased hanging geranium. The plant was hanging by the garage door (which went up and down many times a day), and I worried for them throughout egg-laying, hatching, and launching—all through rain, wind, and hot sun. Watering my plant was a hassle, but it did not seem to deter progress. The wren nest is built like a baby carriage with a hood over it to protect the young, especially from the sun."

Olive Rhines notes another handy nesting site at her former place in Glastonbury, Connecticut: "In our old barn, which provided in the tool room many nooks and crannies, they chose a berry box placed on one of the low side beams. With a great burst of energy, they completed in a few days their nest of twigs, grasses, strips of soft bark, moss, and feathers. The outside was rough and untidy. It was roofed over, with a round opening on the side, leading into a neat, cozy inner chamber. Access to the barn was gained through open windows in the peak, but during the nesting period we left a door ajar for their convenience. Four eggs were soon laid, and although I tried not to interfere with their domestic affairs, my occasional presence never seemed to disturb the sitter-on-the-nest."

Pairs generally raise four to seven young, the male feeding the female on the nest while she's incubating and brooding. The late Arthur A. Allen, world-famous ornithologist at Cornell University, once observed a male house wren desert a nest, soon followed by the female. A male Carolina wren then took over the rearing chores.

Carolina wrens stay put in a given area through the year, although some young or unmated birds head north as fall approaches. Because these birds feed on or near the ground, deep snow can decimate their numbers; some years see an absence of wrens, where only a few months before they were abundant. Mary Rhoads told of a wren that spent winter nights in her Haddonfield, New Jersey conservatory. The bird ate, drank, bathed, and roosted inside, and even slipped into the dining room for crumbs. These wrens are a perplexing mixture of wariness and boldness—good reasons to like them all the more.

Population and Range

Until the turn of this century, Carolina wrens were rare in New England. Fifty years later, they'd spread to Connecticut, Rhode Island, and Cape Cod. Now they breed sporadically over much of eastern Massachusetts. After several consecutive mild winters, we could see this species nesting near Portland, Maine . . . at least for a season.

• *Journal Notes* •

August 14, 1976

It's tomato-picking time here in Hartsville, Tennessee, where I've spent the last month on a rural farm. This morning I saw a couple of brown thrashers (the 35th species recorded from the front porch), and heard jabbering Carolina wrens. The wrens are basically timid, running mouselike through the tangles, or flitting low just out of sight. But they're also inquisitive: if I make a squeaking sound, they're always the first bird to appear. I hope to find one of their nests in a thicket near the tobacco barn, assuming I'm not stopped by ticks, chiggers, or the dreaded poison-ivy. It won't be easy. I might have to wait for leaf-fall.

Blue-gray Gnatcatcher

Polioptila caerulea

This is the only small, gray bird with a black tail bordered by white. Its generic name, *Polioptila,* is from the Greek, meaning gray-feathered; the specific name, *caerulea,* is Latin for sky blue. (Cerulean is a word still used today, meaning deep blue or azure.)

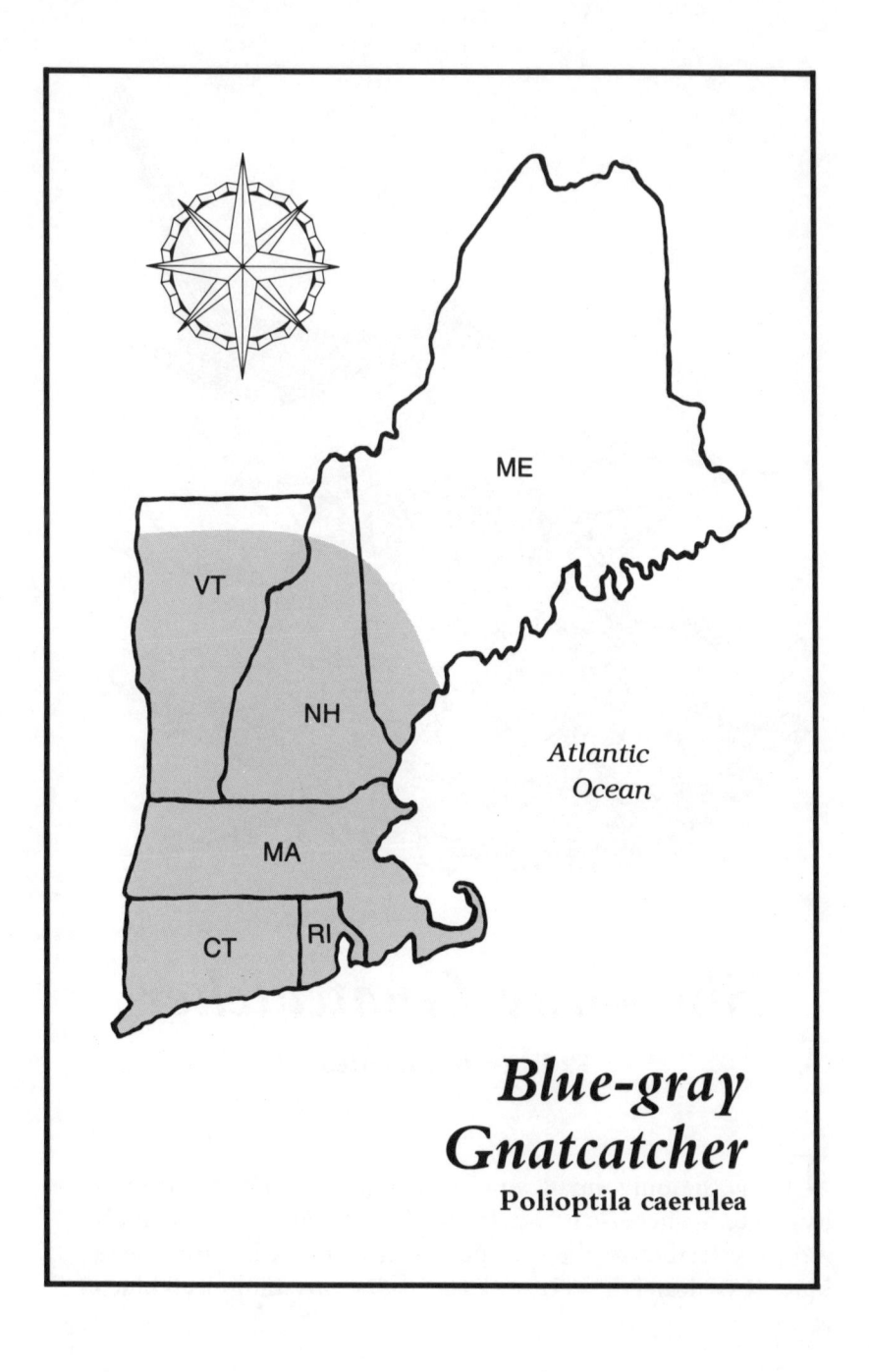

ME

VT

NH

Atlantic
Ocean

MA

CT

RI

Blue-gray
Gnatcatcher
Polioptila caerulea

Field Guidelines

The blue-gray gnatcatcher has the overall appearance of a miniature mockingbird, only more fidgety. At four and a half inches long it's smaller than a chickadee, and is grayish above and white below, with white eye rings. The long tail is often cocked like a wren's, constantly moving both side to side and up and down.

Songs are thin, wheezy, and not easily heard, but the calls—also high-pitched—can be heard by anyone near a nest. This unusual trait doesn't seem to give the nesters away, however, because the nasal scoldings have limited range.

Where tall oaks and pines flourish, and where thickets line quiet streams, gnatcatchers are at home. They hover high and flit around tree flowers and buds, searching for flies, gnats, caddisflies, beetles, and spiders. Treetops are their domain, which they share with pewees and tanagers. Because of this canopy-dwelling habit, and the fact that most other birds are louder, gnatcatchers are easily overlooked. Indeed, beginning birders can go several years before checking off this species, and those who have trouble hearing high notes are at a distinct disadvantage. Gnatcatchers, creepers, and golden-crowned kinglets (all with high, thin calls) make us appreciate the noisier birds; much bird-finding *and* identification is accomplished by sound alone. Birding without hearing is difficult. Early mornings, especially in the spring, are the best times for field trips simply because the birds are at their most vocal.

Gnatcatchers, even in New England, are probably more common than we think: Christmas Bird Counts miss them entirely; the U.S. and Canadian Breeding Bird Survey, which records all birds seen or heard on one morning in June, is too fast a count, and the gnatcatchers would tend to be drowned out anyway; and the Breeding Bird Atlases only record the distribution of the species—not abundance. It's interesting that even in the late-1980s, with legions of birdwatchers scouring the countryside, some species manage to slip by and go about their business undetected. It's also humbling.

Gnatcatcher nests are beautiful, compact cups placed in a tree 5 to 50 feet high on a horizontal branch. Nest materials include catkins, bark, plant down and fiber, and a covering of spider webs and lichens. Like hummingbird nests, gnatcatchers' are extremely hard to find: from underneath, they look like old knots—just a part of the branch. Few people bother climbing trees, inspecting bumps on limbs, even if they know they're getting close. The best way to find a nest is by following birds carrying nesting materials or food. But even this takes patience. Inevitably, however, they give themselves away, leading you right to their home. It's a matter of getting out with binoculars in the spring woods, and quietly listening, watching, and waiting. You can learn so much merely standing still.

With any luck at all (and luck does enter into the game of birding), the waiting will be brief, as Bruce Hedin, of Hancock, New Hampshire, experienced: "On June 5th, 1976, I was rafting with a friend in a cove at Powdermill Pond, when we heard a mystery bird. The next day we identified it as a gnatcatcher when the male came right in, scolding and upset. The female sat on her nest 15 feet over our heads in a young maple tree. It looked like a little gall—part of the horizontal branch—and was covered with lichens on the outside. We didn't bother them much because this was one of the first confirmed nests in the state. For the next few years, I heard them each spring, and even found another nest . . . this one in Hopkinton, N.H."

Nests take a week or two for both birds to build, and they have a strange habit of tearing up half-finished or even completed nests to start another nearby, reusing the old material. Another unusual trait is their waiting 10 days or more after the nest's completion to lay their four or five eggs. Perhaps the delay is to allow leaves to unfold and hide nests even more, but the reason remains unknown.

Paul Roberts, of Medford, Massachusetts, wrote of his experiences with nesting gnatcatchers in the Boston area: "I regularly bird a section of mixed deciduous woods in the spring. Oaks predominate, but frequent brushfires have also created many clearings where blueberries, aspen, birch, and pitch pine dominate. There are few fields. I began birding the area in the mid-'70s, and almost immediately noticed that I was seeing blue-gray gnatcatchers fairly frequently, certainly far more frequently than the birds were generally reported in the records. I had several advantages: these woods are not far from the coast, so that it is relatively warm and acts as a land trap during migration. Even more important, I regularly went out in April.

"Every spring during the last half of the '70s, I saw at least several gnatcatchers in these oak woods. The birds were easily heard and then seen. In early May, it was quite easy to identify nesting territories. The birds never seemed to range very far away from the nest site. On several occasions, before the trees leafed out, I was able to observe nest building, usually in the crook between branches fairly far out on the canopy, and some 20 feet high. The nests were very small and *totally* obscured from ground observation once the trees leafed. Over a period of four years, I could not confirm successful nesting, despite frequent visits to the area. Concern about nesting success was increased because I didn't record increases in total numbers of gnatcatchers observed in late May or early June. Rather, if anything, the numbers actually declined, and I was never able to confirm a significant population increase from one spring to the next. My inclination was to believe that nesting was not very successful, but I could not explain why. Finally, however, in the fifth year, I did observe a pair of gnatcatchers feeding just-fledged young."

Individual pairs differ in the degree of tolerance shown humans near nests; some birds ignore intruders, while others panic. Samuel Grimes once wrote about an attack while he was photographing a nest in Florida. The male " . . . struck the writer several times on the head and once in the eye." (Grimes was temporarily blinded.) On the whole, of course, gnatcatchers are harmless as long as no one bothers them. All wildlife should be treated with respect, and at a respectful distance.

Cowbirds, which lay their eggs in other birds' nests, sometimes victimize even the little gnatcatcher, and blue jays also present problems, as Samuel Grimes notes: "When the jay alighted on the rim of the nest, the gnatcatchers were frantic and darted wildly at him, though they never actually struck him. Unperturbed, they jay grasped an egg in its beak, and flew to a limb some 20 feet from the nest. I watched three trips to the nest, one egg being taken each time. I am inclined to believe that the jay did not take all the eggs, for usually their nest is pulled apart after the last egg is eaten. And on the third visit, the robber appeared annoyed with the continued attacking of the owners, and flew with the egg to a tree before stopping to eat it. He did not return to the nest."

Population and Range

Gnatcatchers are expanding their range northward, especially in Vermont and New Hampshire, but they're still largely absent in Maine and on Cape Cod. They're more common in southern New England, where they reside from late April through October. Until the 1950s gnatcatchers bred only as far north as New Jersey, and even fall wanderers to southern New England were rare. Considering the species' aggressiveness, hardiness, and preference for the type of habitat that northern New England offers (mixed woodlands), it is expected that only mountainous, coniferous forests of the Far North will halt the spread of the sassy ones.

• *Journal Notes* •

July 12, 1980

Gypsy moth caterpillars and pupae are evident on some birches in Needham, Mass. It looks like an invasion year, and writing of invasions, I also saw three blue-gray gnatcatchers at Cutler Park today. Two adults were perched on both sides of a fledgling—alternating feeding. Caring can be violent: the parents crammed insect gobs down its gullet with powerful, swift strokes, almost knocking the youngster off the branch. Too bad gnatcatchers aren't like cuckoos in favoring hairy *caterpillars; if they were, they'd be roving like gypsies, on the trail of those notorious gypsy moths.*

Northern Mockingbird

Mimus polyglottos

The northern mockingbird belongs to the family *Mimidae,* which also includes catbirds and thrashers. All are imitators of other birds' songs, but the mocker is the most versatile mimic of the group. Even its scientific name—Greek for many-tongued mimic—indicates its talents. "Listen to the mockingbird," indeed; America's nightingale is such a great singer that young birds were once caught and caged to liven up living rooms. Ernest Hemingway once praised them, saying "You can play Bach on the phonograph and they will give it right back to you, cadenzas and arias."

Field Guidelines

Gray, slim, and long-tailed, the mockingbird also has white patches on the outer wings and tail, which it flashes during courtship and in flight.

They have their own songs, which vary among individuals, but mockers are most famous for imitating other birds, and even mechanical sounds such as a rusty wheelbarrow axle. Each phrase is repeated several times before switching over to the next. Females sing almost as well as males, nighttime included. There doesn't appear to be any purpose in this night-singing; perhaps in this case one could anthropomorphically say they sing for the pure joy of it. From an elevated perch during spring, summer, and even into the fall, mockers let loose streams of musical and occasionally grating phrases that increase in loudness and tempo, slow down and rise again to ecstatic crescendos. Sometimes a singer actually lifts off its perch in the act, as if totally carried away by the performance—just as a rock singer struts and jumps around the stage in a sweaty frenzy.

Besides songs the birds have assorted calls and notes, uttered during the fall when they are still defending territories. The most common call is a loud, emphatic *Chack!* Eliot Taylor informs me that "the Massachusetts Audubon Society put out a recording of a mockingbird in the town of Weston that could imitate over 30 other species of birds, including a whippoorwill and a flock of blue jays. I *jokingly* tell people that I have played my Peterson's 'Field Guide to Bird Songs' tapes to my mockingbird, and that he imitates them very well. He sits in the bushes and clearly whistles, 'Page 222, hermit thrush . . . ' "

Look and listen for the mockingbird in residential areas, farmland, and thickets at edges of woods. Wherever multiflora roses are planted (especially around shopping plazas), the birds will likely be seen, for rose hips are favorite winter fare. Other cold-weather foods include the fruits of barberry, Virginia creeper, holly, and hackberry. Summertime insects taken in-

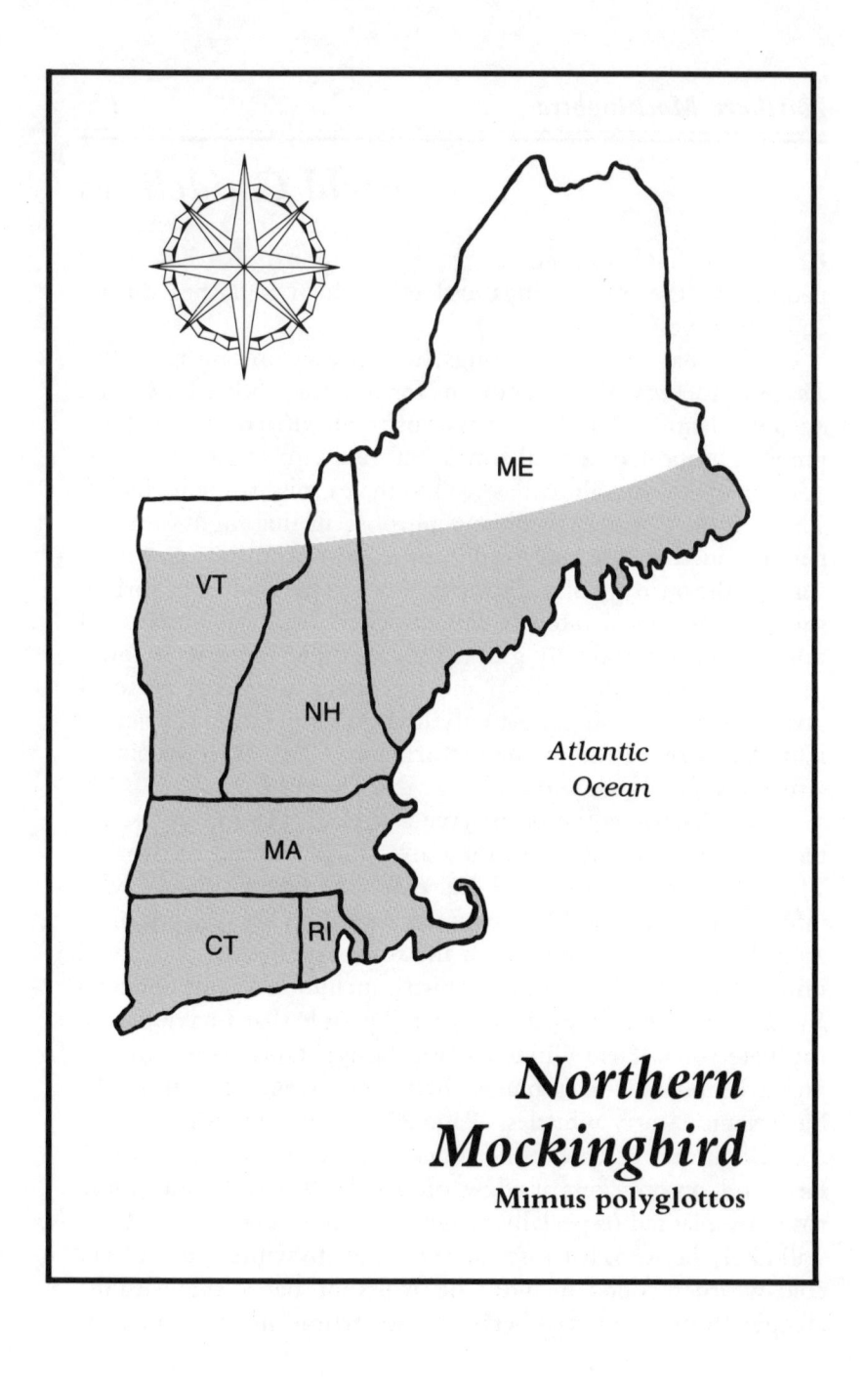

ME

VT

NH

*Atlantic
Ocean*

MA

CT RI

Northern Mockingbird
Mimus polyglottos

clude grasshoppers, beetles, bees, caterpillars, and ants. Mockingbirds, strangely, defend their fruit trees even beyond the breeding season, and they're doubly belligerent toward cedar waxwings. U.S. Forest Service employees in the early 1980s in Alabama witnessed a mocker forcing a waxwing to the ground and pecking it to death. They also found two other punctured waxwing carcasses nearby. The mocker is one species that doesn't lose its spunk after raising a family for the season.

Any time from April through June, a male will sing lustily and circle up in the air until a female appears within his territory. Chasing ensues and the male's singing declines. Both mates help build the twig/leaf/bark nest, which is usually placed in a vine or bush 4 to 10 feet high. During spring and summer mockers become bolder toward people and pets, as seen in this account by Jeanne Friswell: "Around our first house in Holliston, Massachusetts, we had many shrubs, and we were pleased to discover a pair of nesting mockingbirds in one just after we moved in. These expert mimics would fly to the tops of the highest trees on our lot and conspicuously sing their repertoires—as if to let the world know how thrilled they were with *their* new home. Our family cat, a Maine coon named Smokey, studied them all summer, trying unsuccessfully to find their well-hidden nest. In the hottest part of August, Smokey began getting too close to the nest, and suddenly one 100-degree day, as he slowly sauntered across the scorched lawn, the female mockingbird dove down and relentlessly pecked Smokey's back with her long bill. Smokey was startled, but just too hot to object, so he took the abuse.

"Day after day for two weeks, both male and female mockers dive-bombed Smokey, pecking him in the same spot in the middle of his back, until it was raw and almost bald. Smokey finally took the hint and with a flick of his tail, changed his daily prowl to our back woods. The new parents enjoyed the rest of August in peace, raising their brood without the concern of feline threats. And Smokey staked out a new territory."

Three to six eggs are laid per clutch (there are often two broods), followed by a 12-day incubation period. Nestling and fledgling stages are reported by Ruth Buckley, of Needham, Massachusetts: "On June 16, 1984, three mockingbirds hatched in a nest in an arborvitae off our front porch. Both parents fed the babies, paying no attention to us, but were more wary of other people walking by the nest. They chased any other bird away, even chickadees. On June 28th, all three were out of the nest, but only one was out of the tree. A day later, at about 5:00 p.m., one fell to the ground and the parents coaxed it across our side lawn (40 to 45 feet) to a dogwood, where the first baby already was. The mother bird stretched her wings and so did the baby, but he wouldn't fly. A couple of hours later, the mother coaxed the third fledgling across the lawn and into the dogwood tree. The next day we watched the mother forcing one to fly 12 feet, from a bush to a tree. Parents and babies stayed in our yard for about two weeks upon fledging—often returning to the nesting site, with parents still feeding the young."

Because of fierce territoriality, mockingbirds even attack their own reflections in mirrors, windows, and hubcaps, occasionally injuring themselves. M.G. Vaiden reported in Bent's *Life Histories* series: "In June, 1933, my car was parked when I observed a mockingbird pecking at the highly polished radiator. This continued for an hour or more until I moved the car. The next day I noticed the bird doing the same thing, and covered the radiator with a towel to prevent any possible damage to the mocker."

Population and Range

Until about 1950, mockingbirds were rare north of Long Island. By the late '50s they had increased significantly in Connecticut, and by the time Armstrong, Aldrin, and Collins landed on the moon mockers had firmly colonized new frontiers of their own:

the Bay State. Now, in the late '80s, the birds are permanent residents north to southern Canada, and are increasing in the Maritime Provinces. Between 1979 and 1986, New Hampshire's annual February survey revealed that mockingbird numbers doubled, thereby confirming suspicions that northernmost individuals only partially migrate.

There could be a link between the spread of multiflora roses and mockers, according to *Audubon* magazine: the rose was introduced to the United States in the 1870s, but its New England spread didn't begin until the late 1930s, when the Soil Conservation Service planted some for wildlife cover and erosion control. The roses provide year-round benefits for birds: food, cover, and potential nesting sites. Mockingbirds are very much identified with these roses, but considering that the birds range farther north than the plants do the connection isn't positive. It's interesting linkage, nonetheless.

If aided by a succession of mild winters, mockers should increase along the Maine coast and on inland farms. Feeding stations stocked with nuts, raisins, and suet provide additional enticement for this formerly southern species that's now a bonafide Yankee.

• *Journal Notes* •

May 22, 1978

Cemeteries make good birding spots, day or night. They're quiet, open, and handy stopovers for migrants traveling through cities.

At 1:45 this morning, under a full "flower moon," I heard some of the best mockingbird renditions from Holyhood Cemetery in Brookline, Mass. He (or she) imitated about a dozen other species and a barking dog. The notes echoed between the gravestones, which also reflected eerie

*moonlight off polished marble and granite. As I was leav-
ing, I turned intuitively, and saw the silvery wings aflight,
giving life to an otherwise lifeless scene. Birds are where you
find them, whether in the familiar backyard or in a foreign
graveyard.*

Eastern Bluebird

Sialia sialis

The beloved bluebird, known for its color, song, and for heralding spring, is our only blue bird with red on the breast.

When the Pilgrims landed in Massachusetts, there were few bluebirds in that extensive timberland, but by the mid-1800s they were common. At the turn of the century, however, following reforestation and the introduction of house sparrows and starlings, these thrushes declined. Overall, though, populations have increased during the past three centuries, and the birds are currently on another upswing, thanks to the people who put out special bluebird nesting boxes.

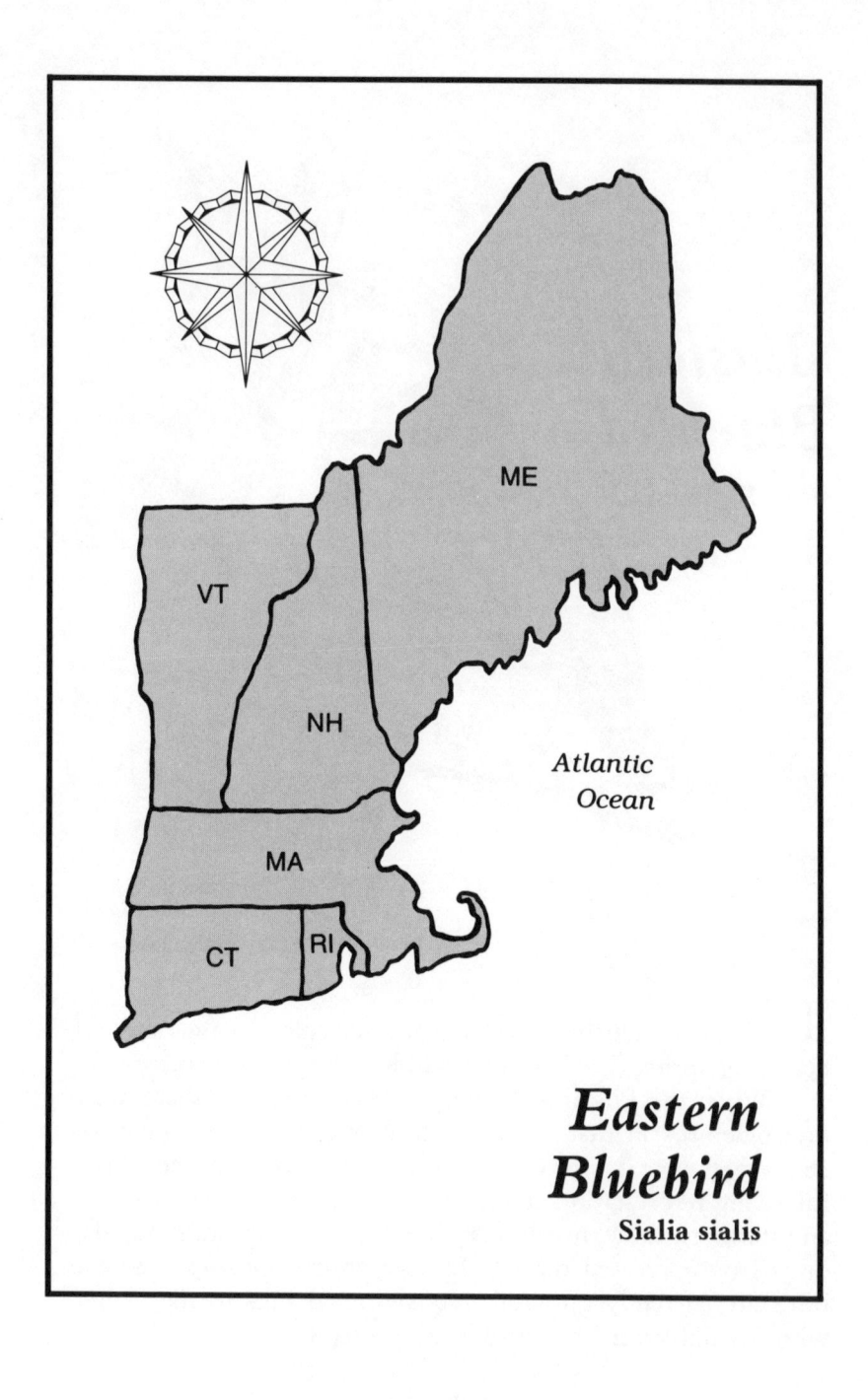

ME

VT

NH

*Atlantic
Ocean*

MA

CT   RI

*Eastern
Bluebird*

Sialia sialis

Field Guidelines

The male bluebird is unmistakable, and the female is a duller blue version. Both appear stooped or round-shouldered when perched; their silhouettes are diagnostic from afar.

Songs are sweet, melodious, almost plaintive warbles that seem to warm up the coldest March day. For many farmers, the spring season begins not with a calendar date but with the first arriving bluebird singing from the telephone wires.

Roadsides, orchards, farmland and open country in general entice this species to spend summers in New England. During the warmer months, bluebirds hunt for May beetles, ground beetles, grasshoppers, crickets, caterpillars, and moths. They alternately catch insects on the wing and by pouncing to the earth. In cold months, when insects are dormant, they eat the fruits of sumac, bayberry, dogwood, Virginia creeper, and multiflora rose.

Males arrive a few days before females, and any time after late April four to six pale blue eggs are laid in the first of two clutches. Originally the birds nested inside dead trees or stumps (especially apple trees), or in a snag at a beaver pond, but now most pairs use birdboxes. Nests of this beautiful species are anything but beautiful; they're loose cups of grasses, weed stalks, and often pine needles. The female alone does the building in the relatively short time of three to five days. She is also an accomplished fighter when defending her brood—even more aggressive than her mate. Both do the feeding, flying low over the ground, then up to the box and inside. For box-nesters that live under our noses, they stealthily come and go right behind our backs.

Raymond Sprague, of Hillsboro, New Hampshire, wrote of nesting-site selection on his property, with some rewarding observations: "I have been fortunate in having had at least one pair of bluebirds nest close to one of my residences for over 30 years, with but one or two exceptions. I have always been amused by the 'How to do it' manuals which insist that bluebird houses shall be built to rigorous specifications; so many inches wide, so many inches deep, hole just so, etc. My observation is that the rattier the house, the more it appeals to some bluebirds. We have a box right on the side of our own house that has been favored by a pair of bluebirds the past two years. This particular bird house was originally designed for wrens some years ago. The squirrels have chewed the entry hole to about a two-inch diameter. A raccoon has practiced housewrecking on it, and if it were a human habitation, it would be swiftly condemned. Some years ago, Exxon gave out little bird houses constructed out of what seemed to be cardboard. They were about four inches square and designed for nothing in particular except to be given away with the purchase of gasoline. A farmhand working for me brought one home, stuck it up about 18 feet in the air on a piece of pipe, and it was *immediately* occupied by a pair of blue-birds that had been hanging around acting choosy."

Thelma Babbitt, a seasoned New Hampshire birder who spends considerable time watching and guarding her birdboxes, wrote of bluebirds' persistence: "For the past two seasons, a pair of bluebirds has come to my yard in the spring and used several of the nesting boxes. In 1984 they built in box #4 near the vegetable garden. After the female had been brooding several days, I noticed them both going in and out of box #5 in back of the house. This seemed strange, so I investigated box #4 and found the nest had no eggs and evidently had been robbed the night before.

"This #5 box is the oldest one I have and was not built to Audubon specifications, although the hole is the required 1^1/$_2$ inches. I didn't realize at the time that the box was not attached securely to the post. The female immediately began building a nest in this box—on top of an abandoned tree swallow nest. She had laid four eggs and had been brooding several days. One morning I looked out, after a violent thunderstorm and high winds, to see the box had fallen off onto the ground. Both bluebirds were nearby in an old apple tree. I dashed out with new screws and screwdriver, and put the box back on the post. It had four newly-hatched birds in it. I watched anxiously to see what the adults would do. Soon both were going in and out of the box feeding the young, and three of the four nestlings were eventually fledged. "

Major bluebird enemies are cats, raccoons, snakes, and house wrens (who puncture the eggs), but particularly Old Man Winter. During the late winter of 1895, severe ice storms hit the southern states, killing thousands of robins and bluebirds. In 1940, a similar catastrophe occurred. Most recently, albeit to a lesser degree, the mini-blizzard of April 6, 1982, dumped 20 inches of snow on the Northeast, killing many migrants who figured the worst was behind them already. Early ground-feeders such as robins, woodcock, and bluebirds are helpless when food supplies are covered and they die en masse, huddled in frozen misery. Fortunately, late snowstorms aren't an annual phenomenon, and within a few years after such disasters they bounce back to previous levels. Usually.

Population and Range

Bluebirds were still common in New England until the 1950s, when woodlands were taking over old farms and DDT did its insidious poisoning job. In addition, competition from starlings and house sparrows for nesting sites presented a problem which still lingers today. It has been estimated that from 1940 to 1980 the eastern bluebird population declined about 90%. Since 1975, however, there's been a slow increase, mainly because of nesting-box programs. The North American Bluebird Society, with nearly 5,000 members, has led the drive to restore bluebirds by erecting boxes all along rural roads in suitable habitats. The Society also provides detailed directions on how to build and install the boxes to bluebird specifications: entrance hole one and a half inches wide (to discourage starlings); no perch (to discourage sparrows); placement on a pole four to eight feet high. As Mr. Sprague mentioned, however, bluebirds will use any old box providing that it's in the right habitat and is relatively predator-free. More information is available by sending a self-addressed, stamped envelope to: The North American Bluebird Society, Box 6295, Silver Spring, Maryland, 20906.

Bluebirds' ancestral habitats are still disappearing, but recently golf courses have been found to partially take the place of apple orchards. Individually, we can help by *not* removing standing deadwood from our property. Snags might be insect-harboring eyesores to some people, but they're choice homes for many species of cavity-nesting birds and mammals. Dead trees yield a lot of life.

Bluebirds are increasing in Quebec, but remain only local nesters, from March through October, throughout New England (with a few wintering on Cape Cod). Despite loss of their preferred habitats there's hope for a continued increase in population. Two successfully-raised broods per pair each year can make a difference. So can nesting boxes. This is one species whose future rests literally in our hands. A little know-how and effort go a long way toward bringing back the most popular bird in the East.

• *Journal Notes* •

May 8, 1985

While looking at four bluebird eggs in a nesting box today, I recalled those idle, carefree times of youth. When I was about 10 years old, I joined the new Needham Bird Club, and on my first field trip we spotted a male bluebird on a telephone line. To my awed, untainted eyes, he positively glowed in the April sunlight. And when he warbled and flew away, I wanted to accompany him "somewhere over the rainbow." It was a special, almost magical sight. Even now, decades and hundreds of wildlife experiences later, bluebirds still move me by their winsome ways . . . still connoting happiness. And I've learned that you can't "strive to be happy." You open up yourself and let it come into you, and pass it along to others. I trust I'll never tire of bluebirds and the outdoors; if I do, I'll have finally aged.

Red-eyed Vireo

Vireo olivaceus

Formerly called "greenlets" (for their olive coloration), red-eyed vireos are the only vireos in the Northeast wearing a black and white stripe above the eyes. Another common name is "preacher birds"—because they repeat their monotonous phrases over and over, from May to September. Undoubtedly they sing more than any other bird in a given year.

Although the species is in a slight decline currently, the author feels comfortable including it here: red-eyed vireos are still expanding northward, as far as trees grow, are still establishing new nesting sites in new areas; and are still one of the most common birds found in eastern woodlands. They're bound to bounce back.

Field Guidelines

Sparrow-sized with red eyes, this vireo is olive-green above and whitish below. The white eyebrow is diagnostic.

Songs are long series of sweet, up-and-down notes, each series being separated by about a one-second pause. From high in the treetops the males sing all day, even during steamy dog days when other birds can't be bothered opening their bills—and often at a rate of 50 phrases per minute. In the early 1960s, a Canadian woman reported that a bird started singing a few minutes before sunrise, then sang for the next 10 of 14 daylight hours, calling some 22,000 times. It is possible that this individual bird is representative of the species in its long-windedness.

Birder Eliot Taylor, of Sherborn, Massachusetts, wrote, "I used to call them 'quarter-mile birds' because from mid-May to mid-August you could hear them every quarter-mile in Massachusetts. (If you ever hear two at once, you have red-eyed stereos.)"

Paul Roberts wrote of his early—often frustrating—days of birding, and of the elusive red-eyed vireo: "Around 1970, when my wife and I were just beginning to develop our interest in birds, we had difficulty differentiating a tree swallow from a blackpoll. Those little birds all looked alike. On a hot summer day, we would occasionally drive to a moderately large freshwater lake in central Massachusetts to enjoy its cool, clear waters and small, shady beach. On weekends, the beach was often crowded, so we would plant our blanket farther up on the grass, next to the swampy scrub and some very old, tall oak trees. While we lay there reading and soaking up the sun, we kept

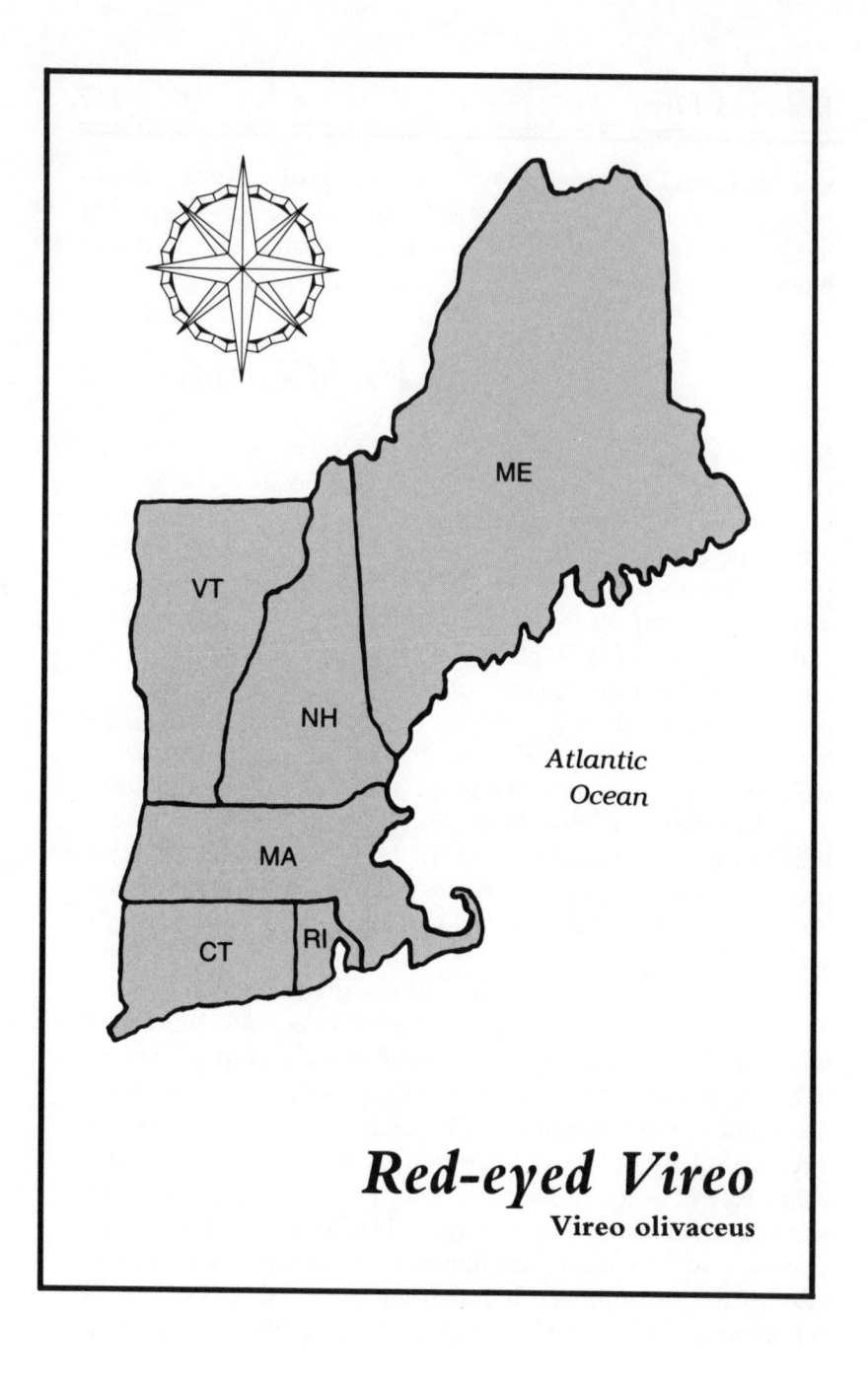

ME

VT

NH

MA

CT RI

Atlantic
Ocean

Red-eyed Vireo
Vireo olivaceus

hearing the same sound—something that sounded like a bird song. I'd take my binoculars over to the tree (perhaps 60 feet high), from whence the sound came. Scanning the tree, not a bird could be seen. The foliage wasn't extremely thick; I just couldn't see any bird moving up there. The song, however, continued as though someone was playing a loop tape. Weekend after weekend, we heard that song. Only when we went on a field trip with some more experienced birders, who heard the same song and identified it for us, did we realize that we'd been hearing red-eyed vireos. They told us that the bird was not very active in the canopy, and was thus more difficult to observe. Were they right!"

As Paul Roberts mentioned, these vireos are canopy-dwellers, whether in a deciduous forest or residential shade trees. They hunt insects deliberately yet not silently; they sing even while flitting after ants, bees, beetles, caterpillars, or moths. With autumn's approach the birds rely more on vegetable matter, including the fruits of dogwood, Virginia creeper, spicebush, and sassafras.

Red-eyed vireos are some of the latest arrivals to nesting grounds in the spring, appearing after bloodroots have started to bloom, and as dreaded black flies increase around central New England. Males arrive shortly before females (to establish breeding territories of about one acre in size), and chase them aerially, fanning their tails and emitting a variety of harsh calls.

While the male sings and watches from a nearby perch the female builds a beautiful, durable nest usually of grass, birch bark, and rootlets, decorated on the outside with lichens. It is interesting that a treetop-dwelling species places its nest so low—about 5 to 15 feet up at the end of a horizontal branch, attached in a fork by spider webbing. The well built, temporary homes cling for years in the trees, and are some of the most commonly seen after leaf-fall. White-footed mice often utilize abandoned nests, enlarging and adding a dome of moss, grass, hair, and feathers.

Two to four eggs are laid in late May or June, depending on latitude, and are all too often accompanied by parasitic cowbird eggs. The female vireo alone incubates for about 12 days, while her mate feverishly sings his heart out. After 10 days in the nest the young birds fledge, but are still fed by both parents for an unusually long time, often through August, well after they attain adult plumage. By late September most vireos have left for interior South America.

As with all wildlife, there are individuals out there, and the following vireo is no exception: Arthur Williams, in 1934, ". . . noticed a red-eyed vireo plunging into a shallow pool of water at the edge of a woodland brook. This unusual behavior was repeated several times. The bird would work down a small branch until it was about eight inches above the water. Here attention was fixed at a certain spot in the water below, and shortly the bird would dive in head first as a kingfisher does. It would then fly to a perch in a tree, and eat something apparently captured from the water. Once, the bird was nearly submerged and had to stop to shake the water off its plumage before eating the morsel." (Moral: the clever bird gets the worm.)

Population and Range

Since the 1940s vireos have been extending their breeding range northward, mostly in the Maritime Provinces, and especially in Newfoundland. Their current range encompasses all of New England, wherever broadleaf trees grow.

• Journal Notes •

July 1, 1971

Vireo nests are normally hard to find except in wintertime, but occasionally you stumble upon surprises even if your mind is elsewhere. Take this morning, at Camp Chewonki in Wiscasset, Maine: I approached the front door of the infirmary, spying a little bird leaving its nest. Looking closer, I counted three white eggs speckled with some black dots at one end. Redeye.

Serendipity seems to occur wherever I go, simply because I'm outside a lot. I don't expect Lady Luck to accompany me forever, but I'll always be open to her. All you need is a pair of open eyes, and the attitude that nature is there to share and to learn from—not overcome. Humans are merely living things like everything else out there. More of us should be humbled by the miracle of life every day, whether it's a chipmunk scratching itself, or a vireo nesting at our doorstep.

December, 1986

In the years since 1971 red-eyed vireos, along with other songbirds such as wood thrushes and some of the warblers, have somewhat declined, apparently due to the loss of winter habitat in neotropical regions. I hope some of the extensive forestland in Central and South America is left untouched; if not, more migratory birds will suffer. Their survival hinges on those hot tracts of balsa, mahogany, and pine so far away from New England.

Prairie Warbler

Dendroica discolor

This member of the wood warblers is the only one that is all yellow below with a striped face. Its specific name, "discolor," is taken from the Latin, meaning parti-colored, and is relatively accurate. The common name, however, is a misnomer; the species barely ranges west to the true prairies, and overall is an inhabitant of brushy country.

Field Guidelines

Prairie warblers are olive-colored above and bright yellow beneath, with distinctive black stripes along the flanks and face. They bob their tails up and down, as do palm warblers, but the best way to positively identify the species—even at a distance—is by the song. From overgrown pastures, pine-oak scrubland, and power line cuts prairie warblers sing long, buzzy series of *Zees* that noticeably ascend the scale. These songs are loud, distinctive, and easily remembered, and veteran birders know instantly where to look for the singers: on an exposed branch within 10 feet of the ground.

Eliot Taylor is just such a birder, offering these helpful insights: "As the name implies, these birds like open country, as do indigo buntings and field sparrows. The ski slopes at Great Blue Hill, just south of Boston, have all three species nesting. I look and listen for them along powerline right-of-ways. Once you become familiar with the prairie's rising calls, you can locate them an eighth of a mile away. I have had them come to me by imitating."

Another experienced field man, Paul Roberts, wrote about the prairie warbler's preferred habitat: "I regularly bird a mixed deciduous woods interspersed with frequently-burned scrub that supports aspen, birch, sumac, and blueberries. The prairie warbler is the most commonly seen breeding warbler in these woods. It will sit fairly far out on a branch, singing its upscale song, reminiscent of a ruby-crowned kinglet's. The bird is found only in, or on the edge of, these scrubby areas. You can walk through open woods for hundreds of yards without seeing one. Then, you come to a small clearing that had been burned over several years earlier, where scrub under 10 feet now predominates—and there is your warbler. I've always been saddened by the frequent brushfires in these urban woods, but I've developed a tolerance for them because I've come to realize that

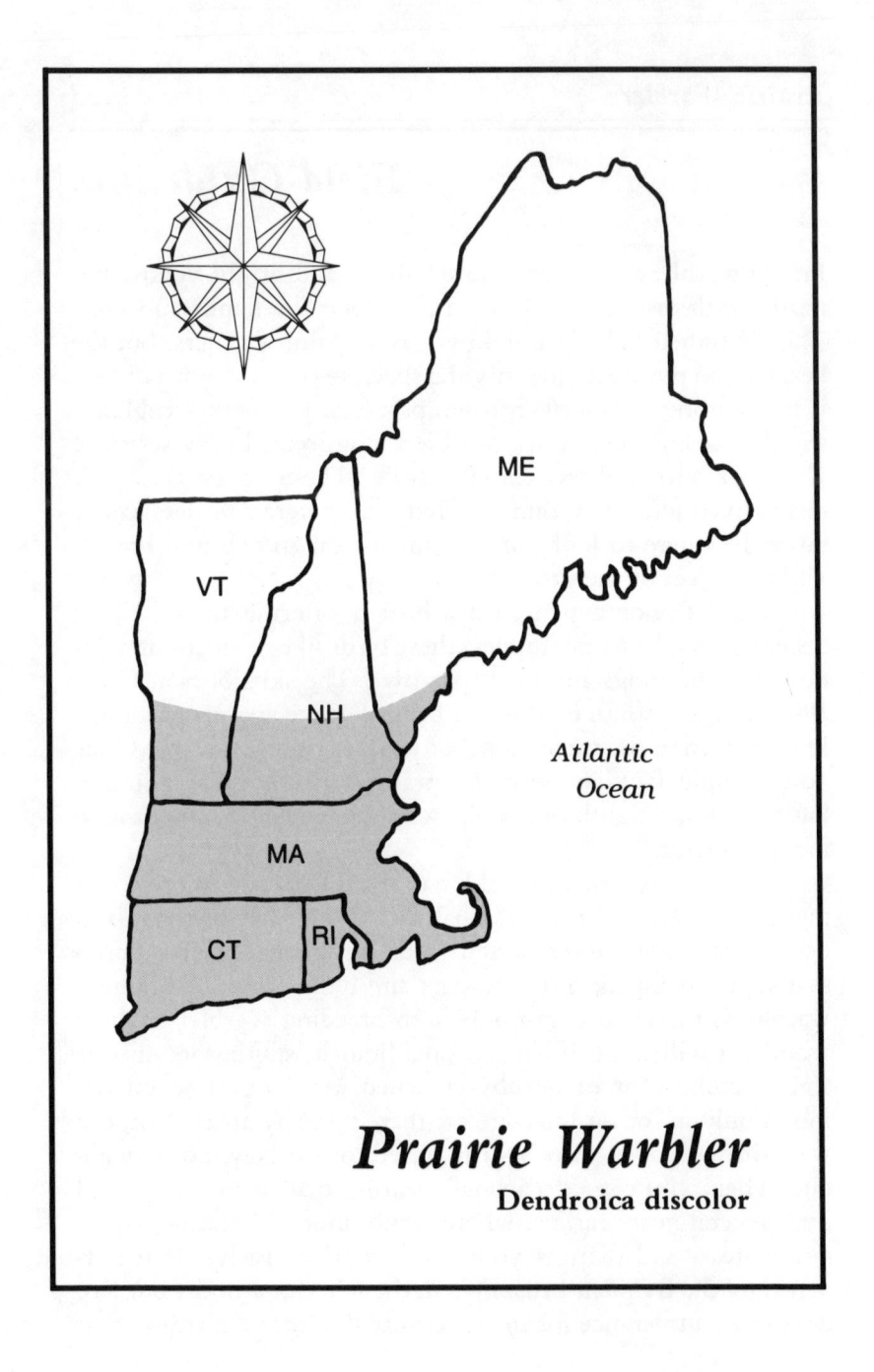

ME

VT

NH

Atlantic
Ocean

MA

CT   RI

Prairie Warbler

Dendroica discolor

without them, I wouldn't have my blueberries or my prairie warblers."

The five-inch birds are very active and acrobatic while catching insects in the air, feverishly fluttering their wings, hovering like hummingbirds, and tirelessly pursuing their prey like a linebacker stalking a quarterback. Their diet is almost exclusively composed of insects, including bugs, beetles, flies, and bees.

Soon after mid-May when these migrants arrive from Central America females begin nest-building—a few feet off the ground and often in briars, bushes, or clumps of sweetfern. The well-concealed cups are made of fine grasses, bark, and plant down, and bound together with spider webbing. Then they're softly lined with hair and feathers. By June, three to five creamy white eggs spotted with brown appear, followed by a two-week incubation period. Come early September, when nighthawks swoop over brilliant swamp maples, prairie warblers of all ages slowly drift toward the mangroves of Florida and points south.

Additional data is needed on this species, but with the dedication and enthusiasm exemplified in the following account, it's only a matter of time. Dr. H. Meade Cadot, an environmental educator from Hancock, New Hampshire, wrote in 1985: "I discovered the prairie warbler about 30 years ago. I was 11 at the time, and finding it was one of my more satisfying moments as a young naturalist. From March to June, I made it a practice to be out by 6:00 a.m. making my rounds before school. Often my route included Valley Garden Park, Delaware, a ten-minute trot as the fox goes, from my house across a field that is slowly being colonized by pines. It was about the first of June when passing one of those pines that I heard what I first thought was an operatic insect. However, I had Peterson's *Field Guide to the Birds* pretty much memorized by then, and the 'Zee zee zee zee zee zee zee zee' flashed through my brain. I crept closer and closer, hoping that my fellow comrades (the family beagles) would stay off on their search for fox or

rabbit scent until I could make eye contact. After what seemed
a quarter of an hour, I was able to line him up in my father's
World War II 6 x 30 binoculars, and BINGO, my Peterson
recollection had paid off: a beautiful male singing away at the
top of a pine.

"I have since heard that song a number of times in the
'prairies' of Virginia, Delaware, and New Hampshire. (In New
Hampshire, the species follows Christmas tree farms and powerline 'prairies' across otherwise seldom-broken woodlands.)
Each time I hear the bird, my mind wanders back to that original sighting in New Castle County, Delaware. When I was
growing up, that county had the fastest growing human population east of the Mississippi. But that field with its pines has so
far survived suburbanization. I hope that prairie warbler's de-
scendants continue to thrive there for the sake of its own kind
and future generations of naturalists."

Population and Range

Prairie warblers were probably not as common a few hundred
years ago—at least in New England. With the cutting and burning of forests to make way for farmland, however, they had
more suitable habitat to breed in. Forest fires can be harmful,
destroying whole plant communities as well as the soil, but light
surface fires can actually increase productivity, and in their wake
increase wildlife populations, including those of deer, moose,
and prairie warblers.

The bushy sproutlands so favored by these warblers are by
nature temporary (overgrowing as quickly as 10 years after a
burn), hence the birds' distribution is spotty and constantly
fluctuating. But here's where man enters the picture, albeit
without regard for the birds: he starts brushfires either by accident or design, blazes lengthy powerlines and maintains them,
and he grows Christmas trees—usually balsam firs—in exten-

sive plantations, particularly in the northern part of the warbler's range, where the birds are expanding. All of these practices create just what this specialized species needs.

Prairie warblers breed across southern New England, nesting locally in most areas and faring even better in the scrub oak-pitch pine barrens of Cape Cod. Northern New England supports limited numbers, the species barely reaching as far as coastal Maine. In the fall, surprisingly, warblers are now regular visitors to regions as far north as Nova Scotia. If current trends in logging, clearing, burning, and the planting of Christmas trees continue, prairie warblers should colonize new boreal territories—just as our own ancestors did over 300 years ago.

• *Journal Notes* •

June 30, 1975. North Truro, Mass.

Walking the fire lane through the stunted pitch pines to work at Head of the Meadow Beach, I heard the familiar rising song of the shy prairie warbler. Just beyond and just above my head perched a male. I stood motionless, my ranger hat in hand, as he pumped his tail, then launched himself up to chase a fly. He swerved to the left, somersaulted down, then caught the fly on the rise. I wondered about the expenditure of energy needed to stay alive. Fortunately for them, there's plenty of prey; fortunately for us, there are birds like warblers to keep the insects in check.

Brown-headed Cowbird

Molothrus ater

The male of this species is the only New England blackbird with a brown head. Formerly called cuckold, lazy bird, and buffalo bird, the brown-headed cowbird is a brood parasite that's often despised for laying its eggs in other birds' nests. Centuries ago it roamed only mid-western plains with the bison; today it covers the entire country and beyond. Many birders still hate cowbirds for chiseling or for being indolent, but one should admire the bird's way of naturally adapting, surviving, and even expanding its range. Are cowbirds really too lazy to build nests, or too smart to bother?

Field Guidelines

The males are seven inches of glossy black with a coffee-colored head, while females are uniformly gray. Both sexes show short, finchlike beaks.

Flight calls are high, squeaky whistles, and songs are bubbly gurgles with a certain liquid quality. Males perform elaborate—and to us, ludicrous—courtship displays on the ground or in the trees, consisting of feather-ruffling, tail-spreading, bowing, and falling forward while "singing" their sputtering notes. Courtships can be easily watched on early spring days because the trees are leafless, and the pairs make considerable movement. Look for these "immoral parasites," as cowbirds have been called through the years, on farms, roadsides, in fields and on the edges of woods. They also come to backyard feeders, where they eat bread, corn, and millet in addition to their normal diet of grasshoppers, oats, and weed seeds.

Cowbirds are unique in North America in that they build no nests, show no brood patches, and defend limited territories. They have been known to lay their four to six eggs in nests of more than 200 species—especially those of warblers, vireos, and finches. At dawn a female will wait until an active nest is unattended, then lay one egg and sneak off, waiting a day to deposit another egg in a different nest. Two or more females have been known to lay an egg in the same nest, forcing a double burden on foster parents.

Reactions by duped birds vary: most accept the strange, often-larger eggs as their own and raise the young; some simply desert the nest; robins and catbirds can detect the trickery, abruptly discarding the foreign objects; yellow warblers usually build new nests right over cowbird eggs, resulting in multi-storied affairs. Because of a short (12-day) incubation period, fast-growing cowbird nestlings have the edge on smaller young, who sometimes starve in fighting vainly for their share.

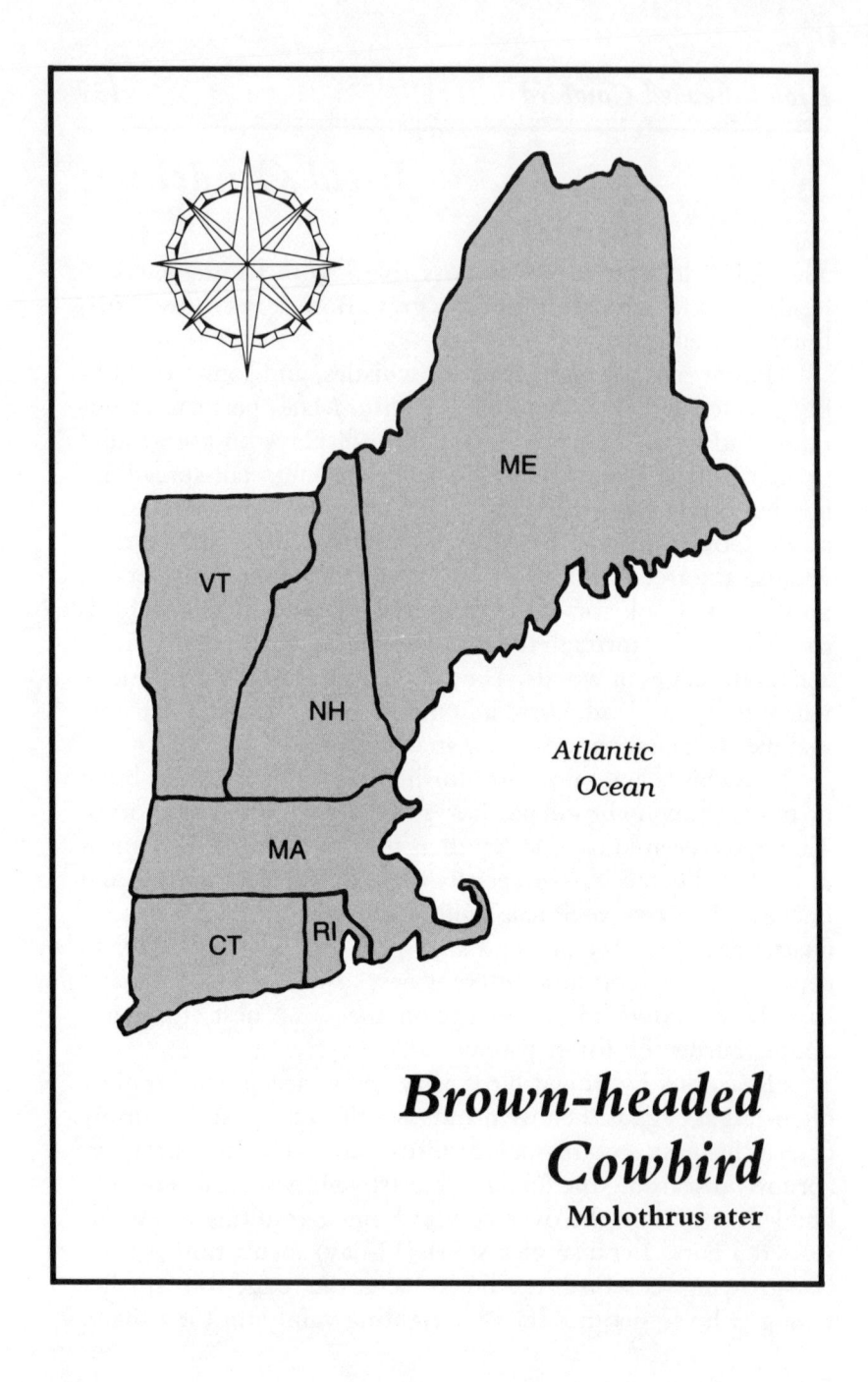

ME

VT

NH

*Atlantic
Ocean*

MA

CT

RI

*Brown-headed
Cowbird*

Molothrus ater

Olive Rhines states that, "There is ample proof of the cowbird winning out. For several days, a female song sparrow that was brought to my porch on the Connecticut shore, fed a baby cowbird almost twice the size of the mother. The foster mother had to stretch with all her vigor to reach up to that cowbird's gaping mouth. A ridiculous performance. There was no doubt that the sparrow's own young had been sacrificed while the unwelcome guest was winner-take-all."

Mary Dickert, of Needham, Massachusetts, wrote: "My first experience with a cowbird was a puffed-up baby sitting in grass, being pecked and pushed around by a mother starling. We rescued the baby with an overturned basket. I suppose it was hatched and fed for awhile by the stepmother starling, who finally forced it to leave the nest."

Canadian environmental educator Mike Zettek describes a natural mystery in the Catskills: "What more could a summer camp naturalist ask for? On my second day of exploring the varied environs of S.U.N.Y./New Paltz's Ashokan Field Campus, I discovered three active phoebe nests. By canoe, I found the third one, well-concealed on the shale wall of a small gorge that had been flooded when the Esopus Creek was dammed. The dutiful parents, intent on feeding newly-hatched chicks, showed me where it was, and I couldn't resist taking a peek inside. (It merely required standing up in the canoe and looking down.) I was startled to find two small chicks, and two that were nearly twice their size. A case of cowbird parasitism?

"I returned the next day to show some young campers, and was shocked to find only three chicks. Now there was but one tiny bird, dwarfed by the other monsters. The next day we mourned the disappearance of the other small nestling. Were we at the scene of a double murder? We were perplexed. All thoughts of a fair and speedy trial went out the window a couple of days later, when we found the nest vacant of all birds. Of one thing I'm certain: cowbirds should keep their distance from those New York boys!"

Young cowbirds, isolated from their own kind, fledge in about 10 days, then join flocks, which indicates an absence of imprinting on the foster parents. (And proving that birds of a feather eventually flock together.) Olive Rhines tells of cowbird populations through the seasons: "My first acquaintance with cowbirds was in the great mixed flocks of blackbirds that annually appear almost overnight along the Connecticut River Valley in late February or early March. Associating closely with redwings, grackles, and starlings, the cowbird can then be found in great numbers on open, ploughed fields where there is an abundance of weed seeds, insects, and leftover morsels of corn. Most cowbirds migrate south during the cold months, but in the early '50s they began to show up in small flocks throughout the winter in southern New England. My very first lessons in birdbanding during the winter of 1951–52 involved a flock of cowbirds that readily entered the banding traps—lured by mixed seed.

"In nature, the average pair of breeding birds is beset with many hazards in the successful rearing of young to perpetuate its own kind. The imposition of cowbirds in the nesting process is one more threat to a potential brood. The overall success of the cowbirds' parasitic tactics may be seen in the undiminished flocks that populate the countryside within its natural range."

Population and Range

Following the clearing of forests to open areas for crops and livestock cowbirds spread from the plains, settling into new eastern regions. Even areas without cattle now entice the birds; farm grains suffice for food in lieu of rustled-up insects. Similar to real Yankees, New England cowbirds are hardy and adaptive.

Cowbirds are common permanent residents in southern and central New England, and summer residents (late March through October) throughout northern sections. Few individuals stay and survive north of Concord, New Hampshire, except along coastal Maine.

Considering that both sexes are promiscuous, and that females lay two or three "clutches" of eggs annually, there's no concern over the status of the species. Indeed, many people—birders in particular—think that there are already too many of them. But cowbirds are not significantly harmful to other songbirds' population because the hosts are not decimated by these interlopers. There seems to be room in nature for these unique parasites, and it should be remembered that many of us don't build our own houses either, and we also give up some of our offspring to foster parents.

• *Journal Notes* •

May 8, 1985

I found my first cowbird eggs today. Earlier in the day, I'd seen a male and female walking warily on the lawn, tails up in customary posture. Inside an eight-foot-high phoebe nest, attached to the house where I work, were two cowbird eggs and four phoebe eggs. The cowbird eggs (which I removed under the direction of the homeowner) were strikingly different from each other; one was oval with brown spots concentrated at the larger end; the other was long-oval in shape, uniformly dotted with brown. I figured two females had laid them at about the same time.

P.S. All four phoebes eventually fledged. I feel only minimal guilt in pocketing the undesirable eggs; they now decorate my bookshelf, resting beside a vulture skull.

June 23, 1986

Dave Rowell and I went on our second Breeding Bird Survey, ending near Granite Lake in Stoddard, N.H.

After five hours and 50 stops, we needed a pick-me-up. We got it. High in a pine, we spotted a black and white warbler (about five inches long) feeding a fledged cowbird (about seven inches long and much heavier). The little warbler's head nearly disappeared inside that gaping maw. It's ironic that next year the fledgling might very well parasitize its own parent.

European Starling

Sturnus vulgaris

The beautiful and vociferous starling is now so common it's one of the most neglected—even hated—of all birds. When Eugene Schieffelin, a New York entrepreneur, populated Central Park with 40 pairs in March, 1890, all he wanted to do was introduce those species that were mentioned in Shakespeare's plays. (Odd, but true.) Most attempts failed, but not the starlings; by 1898 they had spread to New Jersey and Connecticut. These favorites of Elizabethan courtiers (because of their mim-

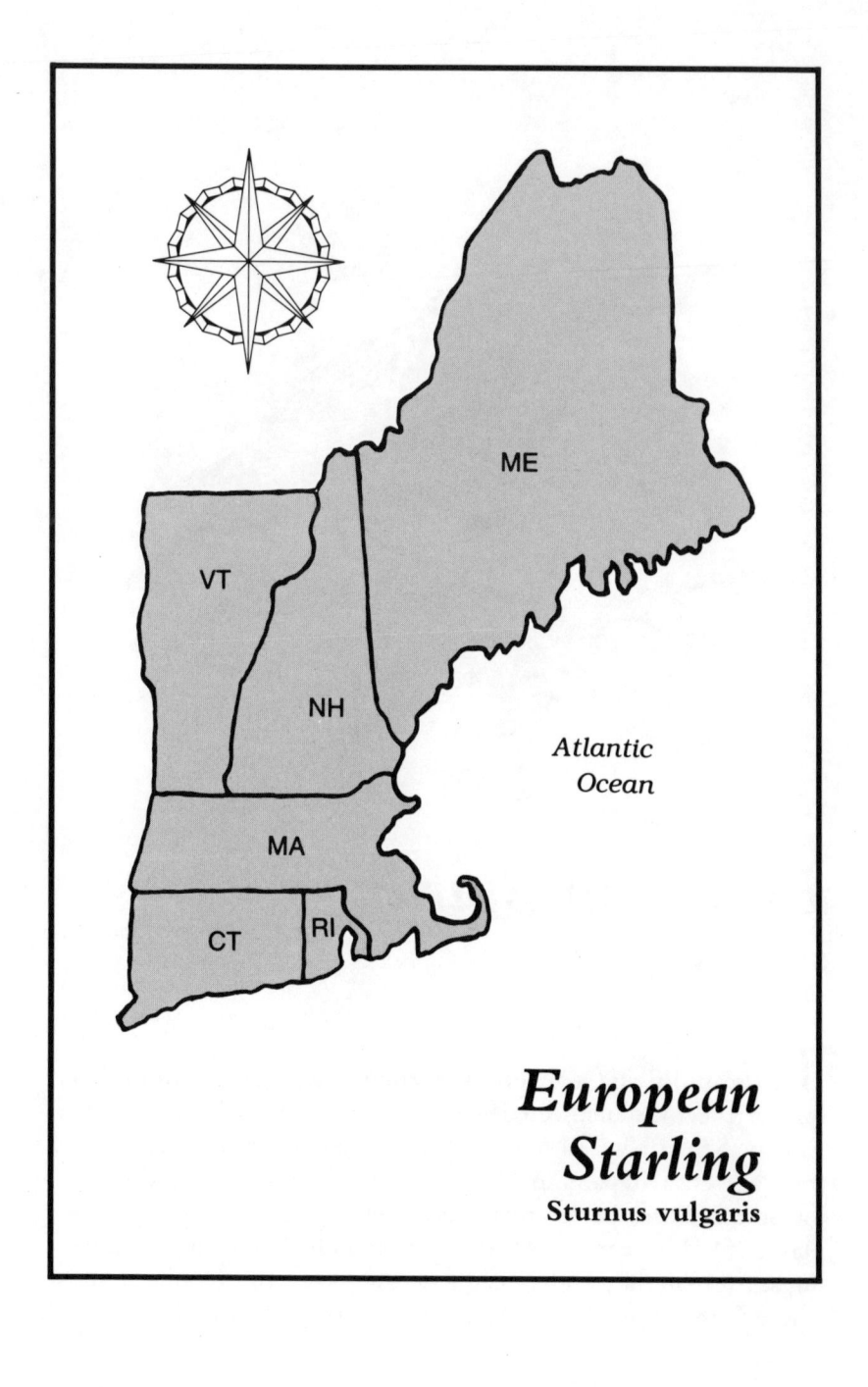

ME

VT

NH

*Atlantic
Ocean*

MA

CT

RI

*European
Starling*

Sturnus vulgaris

icking abilities) are now probably the most populous species in the United States.

Paul Roberts, an expert birder and starling-lover, wrote of how ubiquitous they are near his home in Medford, Massachusetts: "Perhaps more Americans are familiar with the starling than any other bird, though they don't realize it. Every winter, at least one Boston radio station receives numerous phone calls inquiring about what birds are flocking by the thousands over the city. Each fall the starlings roost in a flock estimated at upwards of 200,000 on the girders of the Mystic River Bridge. Rivers of thousands can be seen flying back across the city late every winter afternoon, and people can't help but see these dark, delta-winged silhouettes flowing toward the bridge. Starlings are disdained by many, especially by birders because of their success in driving out other species. This is compounded by the fact that they are so common. Many people feel less interest in, less affection for, something that is thriving."

Margarete Corbo, of Falmouth Heights, Massachusetts, is another rare birder who feels great affection for starlings. In 1983, she wrote a popular book titled *Arnie, The Darling Starling,* which describes her success in teaching the bird to talk, whistle tunes, and drink wine. With people like her, the lowly starling's image just might improve.

Field Guidelines

Both starling sexes look identical: chunky, short-tailed, iridescent, blackish birds with prominent yellow bills. In winter they are heavily speckled with white, and sport dark bills.

Male songs are varied squeals, whistles, and chuckles, mixed with passable imitations of other birds' calls. Starling utterances—some of them grating to our ears—are commonly heard on city streets, suburban lawns, and farms. Sometimes, when large flocks roost near humans, we react like madmen; in

Crawfordsville, Indiana in 1981, people stalked around beating pots and pans to scare off the transient birds. One Alfred Starling, a former Audubon leader, said this crude tactic wouldn't work. He was right.

Voracious eaters, starlings damage our cherry and corn crops, but help us by catching cutworms, weevils, and the dreaded Japanese beetles and gypsy moth caterpillars. They usually feed on the ground (where they walk and waddle about nervously), and also visit feeders, where they oust all other wildlife except squirrels.

Starlings start the nesting season early, courting when maple sap is first rising, and nest-building on the first days of spring. Males wave their wings and fluff out their throat feathers, crowing in muffled tones with closed beaks. Soon pairs work on their nests together, the male forming the base and the female promptly removing much of this to build the final version.

Nest sites are in tree cavities (usually deadwood), bird-boxes, or around buildings. 10 to 30 feet up, the slovenly, befouled nests are made of weeds, grass, corn husks, dead leaves, and a few feathers. Starlings are notorious for evicting other species from their own cavities, including bluebirds, flickers, martins, and wrens. It is fortunate that starlings cannot enter birdhouses with entrances of less than 1 1/2 inches in diameter. At least some of the native cavity-nesters are safe from these immigrants.

Both mates incubate the four to six pale blue eggs for about 12 days, followed by a three-week nestling phase. There are often two broods. In late summer, young and old birds form clamorous, communal roosts that often contain several thousand individuals, usually settling in groves, or on buildings or bridges. Despite the fact that today's office buildings are designed for easy maintenance (with a minimum of nooks and ledges), starlings still find ample roosting sites—a concern to health officials.

Population and Range

Even before World War II, when starlings had spread out from the East to reach the Rocky Mountains, they were a nuisance in the cities. In Washington, D.C., the birds befouled the friezes on government office buildings so much that by the early 1960s Congress considered decimating their feathered neighbors. Even the lofty White House, under President Kennedy, didn't escape avian whitewashing; the National Park Service had to broadcast distressed starling calls on loudspeakers day and night to cut down the increasing numbers of birds and amounts of excrement piling up. And the Electra plane crash at Logan International Airport in October, 1960, which killed 62 passengers, gave starlings an even worse name as they were blamed for innocently getting sucked into the engines and causing the tragedy.

Scare tactics used on starlings and other flocking species usually work only temporarily, or fail altogether. Theoretically, they should be effective *and* safe for humans. Dummy owls placed on ledges, and poison gases swabbed onto buildings, work just so long, but spraying ammonia onto roosting trees on cold nights has proven effective: the birds' feathers freeze, and the luckless starlings soon topple from their perches.

Perhaps the best deterrent is a combination of taped distress calls and either firecrackers or gun blasts. In Brockton, Massachusetts, in August, 1982, an estimated 15,000 starlings roosted in a maple stand, and during their comings and goings, they defiled swimming pools, sandboxes, and clothes on the lines. At dusk city police fired off shotgun rounds into the woods, while health officials simultaneously played starling alarm calls. Within a few nights the birds vanished—albeit to someone else's backyard.

We created starling problems, so we are stuck with solving them, at least at the local level. But do we really have a right to control even undesirable, imported species? Don't birds "belong" to all of us? Maybe it's already too late to debate this issue, for starlings are here to stay, and nothing we do will remove them and their cocky ways.

European starlings are permanent residents throughout New England, although some withdraw southward from far northern sections. They are common to abundant in most habitats except in deep woods and around aquatic environments. They'll keep on leering down at us from manmade structures as long as we exist. Perhaps even longer.

• *Journal Notes* •

September 22, 1979

. . . a rainy evening at Boston's South Station. While waiting for the Amtrak to take me to Nashville, I watched a flock of hundreds of starlings readying to roost. They beat wings and moved in unison, maneuvering as one. As they settled under a bridge, I wondered how such a big flock (apparently without a leader) could stay together. A crowd of humans certainly couldn't duplicate their timing, spacing, or unity. In mobs, people behave irrationally, while starlings remain collectively cool.

House Sparrow

Passer domesticus

The house (formerly "English") sparrow takes its scientific name from the Latin: *passer* = sparrow; *domesticus* = house. Few species have spread so fast and caused such a flap as this little immigrant; it was mainly due to the house sparrow that the Lacey Bill was passed in 1900 forbidding importation of foreign creatures without a permit. By 1985, however, at least one person—a Connecticut legislator—saw fit to protect such city birds as sparrows and starlings from death by bloating. He proposed a bill that would require a $50 fine for throwing rice at weddings. (The bill was thrown out). Other people, of course, would just as soon see all the dirty city-dwelling birds elimi-

171

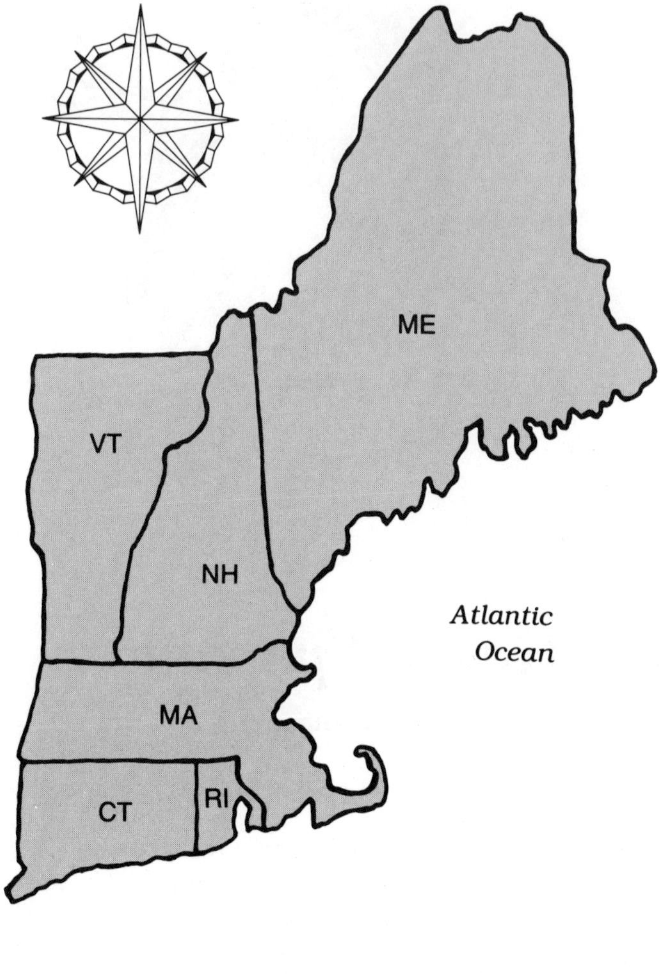

ME

VT

NH

*Atlantic
Ocean*

MA

CT

RI

House Sparrow

Passer domesticus

nated, but the hardy house sparrows will outlive us all, flitting unruffled down the decades.

Field Guidelines

The male's black bib and gray cap, and the female's overall tawny drabness, are known to everyone with eyes. Calls are monotonous cheeps and chirps heard throughout the year in city parks, busy streetcorners, and on the remaining farms in New England.

House sparrows are largely seed-eaters, picking up oats, corn, wheat, and ragweed. In summer they also catch Japanese beetles, May beetles, weevils, and cankerworms. During lean times they wing it over to Easy Street, where they dine on practically anything, including dung beetles and garbage.

Pairs performing their courtship antics in spring and summer are fairly easy to discover. They shake their wings and hop around, chirping repeatedly. Male sparrows, more than most other species, do their fair share of nest-building, and by March the nests are completed—messy, spherical globs up to the size of volleyballs, made of grass, leaves, weeds, twigs, paper, string, and lined with feathers. These are placed in birdboxes, tree holes, awnings, behind shutters, etc., usually from 10 to 30 feet high.

Nests stuffed into gutters and rainspouts can cause problems for householders, but those located behind neon signs can attract nosy naturalists, as New Hampshire's Paul Crowley remembers. "I was about ten years old in Farmingdale, New York, and I saw these little birds flying out from the third story of a brick office building. It was dusk, and I was with a friend. Both of us climbed a lot as youngsters, so up we went along the side of the building, scared but curious as to what kind of birds were up there. As I eased toward the nests, I reached in behind the neon sign, where it was dark. Suddenly birds flew out at my face, almost causing me to lose my grip. I nervously picked my way back down. Later I found out that they were the same birds that ate the rice at weddings: house sparrows. I guess I still like them because they remind me of home."

Four to six eggs are laid per clutch, and often two or even three broods are raised during the long breeding season. After the female incubates for 12 days, and following a 15-day nestling period, the young fledge—usually all on the same day. By late summer large flocks gather to feed and roost together, sometimes traveling several miles to spend nights huddled in defiled vines on houses.

Bygone summer days are fondly recalled in this account from Annette Cottrell of Hillsboro, New Hampshire: "House sparrows spell childhood in another age to me—the age before the automobile and macademized roads; the age of dust, or dubious mud; the age of horses' hooves clop-clopping along as I sat, perched on the hard wagon seat behind the horse's behind. Forward motion was so slow that I had time to look around where we were going. A treeless stretch was dreaded on hot summer days, or the cold wind blowing across it in winter.

"Certain elements were constant: the smell of the leather reins and harness, the smell of the periodic, deliberate delivery of manure from the rear of the horse, and the cheerful cheeping of house sparrows clustering around these heaps down the middle of the road. Little did these birds mind the growing protests from humans. As long as there were horses and barnyards, newly-seeded fields and pastures for stock, they throve. The obligato of my days was the twittering of the sparrows."

Population and Range

In the spring of 1851, eight pairs of imported house sparrows were released in Brooklyn, New York, followed by more during the next few years in Portland, Maine, and Quebec. The result was impressive, and by 1886 these unpopular weaver finches (they're not true sparrows) had reached the Mississippi River. By 1900 they were dispersed across the whole country. They feasted free and fine on oats and other waste grain, as well as horse manure.

But not for long; the times were soon to change, and with them, people's attitudes.

Retired New Hampshire forester Henry Baldwin remembers the old days of about 1910 in this written account: "House sparrows were all too abundant in the horse and buggy era. They were everywhere making dirty nests in eavespouts and roof corners. A doctor down the street at Saranac Lake paid us a penny each for killing them with a BB gun. My father constructed a net frame about eight feet square, upheld on one side by a stick. Grain was put on the ground, and the stick pulled out by a string from a distant window.

"Later, birds were lured by grain for a few days, then the grain was replaced by poison. All these methods (and many more) were outclassed by the skill with which Louis Agassiz Fuertes picked them off his clothesline with a blowgun. As a frequent guest of the great artist, he taught me how to blow . . . but I never hit much."

Adaptable, aggressive, and gregarious, house sparrows quickly drew many people's wrath for ousting native species like bluebirds and swallows from their traditional nesting sites. But by 1930, as roadside waste grain grew scarcer with the rise of the automobile, and starlings competing for nesting sites, the sparrows had imperceptibly decreased anyway to more acceptable levels. Since then the species has faced yet another threat: the house finch. The two species compete not only for nesting sites, but for food, and so far the finches are winning.

House sparrows are common permanent residents throughout New England, especially around farmland and populated areas. It appears that they've reached their population limits, and as farms are developed and woodlands take over, sparrows simply move on, back to the spreading urban centers from where they originated.

• *Journal Notes* •

April 5, 1985

For the past week, my employer has had me cover two of her birdhouse entrances with masking tape to keep out house sparrows until swallows and bluebirds arrive. Today, I removed a bulky sparrow nest made of weeds, grass, toilet paper, string, and hemlock tips. I threw it 10 feet away, and two hours later, half of the same nest was back in the box. It appeared intact, in the same shape, as if the birds had stuffed it inside in one piece. Fast, admirable work. It's too bad these birds aren't wanted except on the most-wanted list; along with the pigeon and starling, the house sparrow is the only species not afforded protection in the United States.

December 19, 1987

Bruce Hedin, Eleanor Cappa, and I just completed the Bennington section of the Monadnock Region Christmas Bird Count. We recorded 21 species, including a northern shrike at day's end. We also saw the usual band of 15 house sparrows in the village. They brought back memories of the sparrows that nested among the ivy and behind the shutters of my old home in Needham, Mass.

I remember sweeping up the droppings covering the back steps, seeing the birds take dust baths on hot summer days, and hearing their garbled racket before roosting for the night. Although house sparrows are considered dirty pests in some circles, I still retain a special fondness for them; without house sparrows I might not have become a birder or a writer.

Northern Cardinal

Cardinalis cardinalis

The cardinal, or redbird, is the only crested red bird in the East. It also has the distinction of holding State Bird status in seven states—all of them outside New England. A member of the large finch family, the cardinal takes its name from the rich red color of Roman Catholic robes.

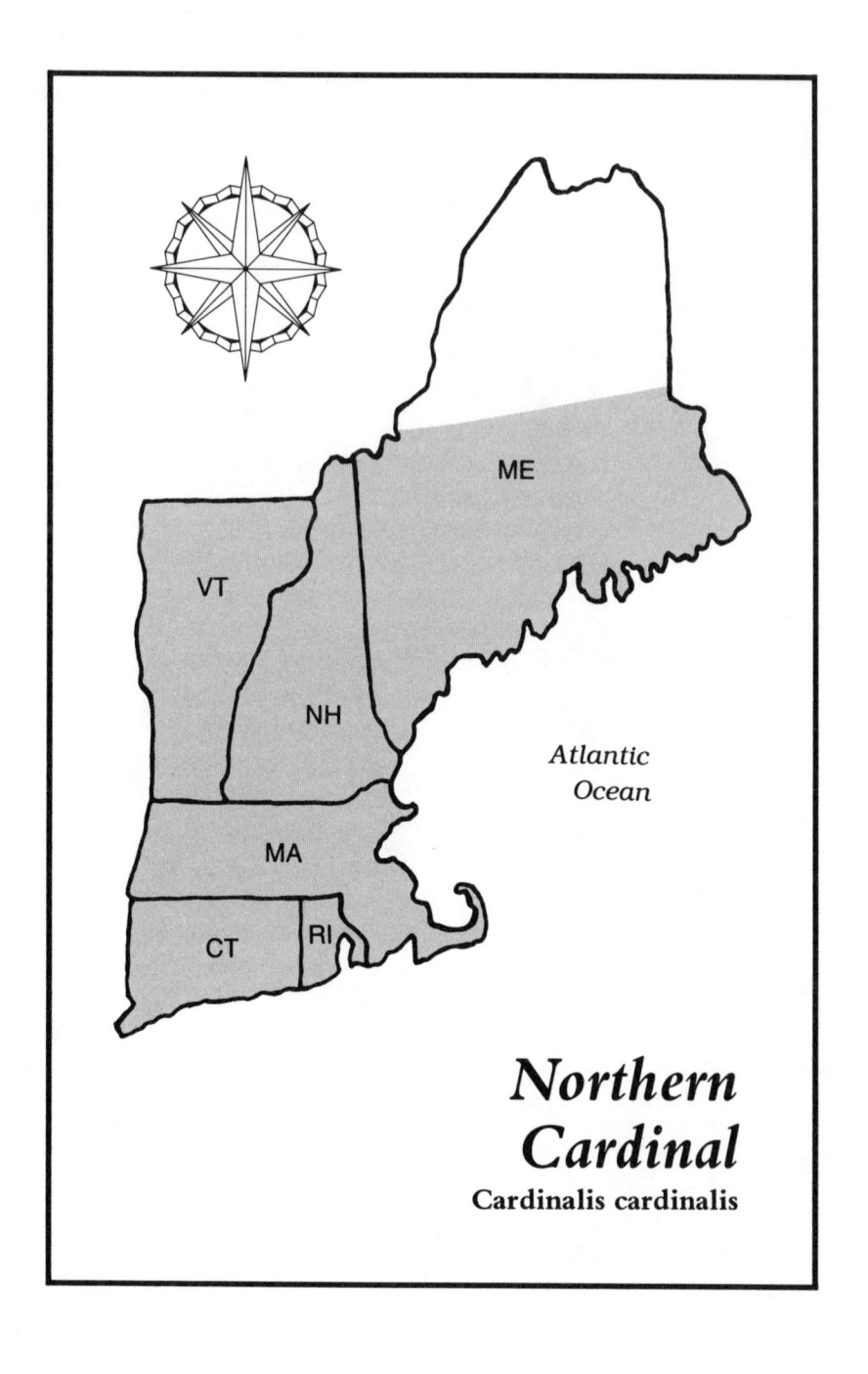

ME

VT

NH

*Atlantic
Ocean*

MA

CT RI

*Northern
Cardinal*

Cardinalis cardinalis

Field Guidelines

Males are unmistakable with their vermilion plumage, black face, and crested head. Females are buff brown with a smattering of red on the tail, wings, and, like the males, the bill. Young birds resemble females except for their dark beaks.

Cardinals are unusual in that both sexes are competent singers, although females have shorter singing seasons. Their songs are loud, clear, piercing whistles that bubble up and fall at the end of each varied series. Calls are sharp chips with a metallic quality, similar to those of rose-breasted grosbeaks.

Deep forests have no allure for these birds; cardinals show off their regal redness in suburban yards, gardens, and thickets along woods borders. Their summer diet consists of insects, seeds, and fruit, and in winter they eat mainly wild grains and choice feeder food such as corn and sunflower seeds.

Paul Russo, of South Yarmouth, Massachusetts, sent this story of his punctual backyard cardinals: "We had attracted several pairs of cardinals, which came to feed before 6 a.m., 10 a.m. and after 3 p.m. One morning about 10, we heard rapping at one of our windows. It was a female cardinal on the back of the patio chair, pecking the window in the Florida room where we usually sit. When we spotted her, she flew to the shrubbery bed and back again to tapping. Could it be that we were being told to get out the sunflower seeds? We thought it was only a coincidence, but to test it, the next day I omitted the sunflower seeds. Sure enough, she was back pecking at the window, while her mate waited on a tree branch. We tried the same plan a week later (omitting the seeds, that is), and yes, she returned to the window, letting us know we had fallen down on our feeding assignment." (Another possible explanation for her behavior is that she saw her reflection; cardinals are notorious for fighting mirrors and windows in defense of their year-round territories.)

The females do most of the nest-building within a week, placing them in saplings, bushes, or tangles of vines. The nests, which resemble those of catbirds, are made of twigs, bark, grass, and vines, and hidden in dense shrubbery up to 10 feet high. A few days after the nest is ready, three to five greenish white and blotched with brown eggs are laid in the first of typically two broods. Following an incubation period of about 12 days the eggs hatch, and 10 days later the young fledge into a world of whirring lawn mowers, buzzing insects, and warm summer breezes. Some birds will drift northward, but most will remain, later adding color to snowy backyards.

Population and Range

Ever since the first Massachusetts nest was discovered in 1957, cardinals have steadily inched northward. Eliot Taylor, of Sherborn, Massachusetts, wrote in 1985, "For 20 years there have been as many as 10 cardinals at a feeder near my house, but it has only been the last few years that they were regular visitors to my yard. I found that early Sunday mornings were the best times to see them in the yard. I guess that my neighbors sleep late, and the hungry birds wander around looking for some full feeders. How any birds can be so local and at the same time expand their range from New York to Maine I don't understand."

Marilyn Mollicone, from Augusta, Maine, writes of her personal experiences: "For me, one of the most exciting birding events of recent years has been the northward spread of cardinals. Some time in the late '50s or early '60s, I was inspired by a magazine article about planting shrubs and flowers for the purpose of attracting specific birds to an area. I vowed, aloud, that I would some day attract cardinals to my yard. A more advanced birding friend went to a great deal of trouble to assure me that it was not going to happen here in central Maine, backing his statements with details of all the cardinals ever sighted in Maine.

"Less than ten years later, I began to hear reports of cardinal sightings coming closer and closer to our area. I saw my first one in 1972 on the Augusta Christmas Count. In the late fall of 1974, I saw them in my own yard at a feeder. That was a red-letter day! Now they are thoroughly established in central Maine and are still moving northward. For several years the parents have brought young to my feeder, and I have seen as many as six in the yard at one time. It is perhaps even more exciting to realize that the cardinal is only one of a number of birds that are extending their ranges in the same manner."

Cardinals have also increased in Vermont, and in New Hampshire the Audubon Society has recorded more and more individuals on their late-winter survey: 556 in 1980, 923 in 1984, and 1,047 in 1986. The current range covers all of New England except northern Maine, although the species has bred in Nova Scotia. As more houselots appear in northern New England one can expect cardinals to extend their permanent range even farther, especially if people continue to feed the birds in winter. (Save those melon seeds.)

• *Journal Notes* •

March, 1971

I saw my first New England cardinal today on a telephone wire in front of our house. I'd never heard one before, but I somehow knew what it was, so I bounded down the stairs and out the door. The male redbird sang mightily, bouncing the bubbly tunes around the neighborhood for all to hear. (Few did, if any.) It's no wonder that in bygone days this species was used as a cage bird. Oh, to hear a duet. It's sure hard to ignore cardinals . . .

House Finch

Carpodacus mexicanus

The house finch, or linnet as it's called out West, is a recent invader and a most explosive expansionist. Originally a western species, but introduced to Long Island, New York, in 1940, it has spread so fast that it could conceivably merge with the western population in the next few decades.

Field Guidelines

Compared to raspberry-colored purple finches, male house finches display *orange*-red on their chest, head, and rump. Heavy brown stripes line the belly. Females and immatures are nondescript—finely streaked in a light brown. All show the seed-cracking, conical bills so prevalent in the finch family.

The song is a long, varied warble that, unlike the purple finch, ends with a rough jeering. Calls, similar to a house sparrow's, are lively yet sad-sounding cheeps. Unmusical chattering rounds out their repertoire.

House finches live among us, and indeed are much like us; most prefer urban life but make regular forays to rural, open country spaces. Wherever humans alter the environment to suit their own needs finches follow and benefit. In New England, these finches are taking up where house sparrows left off after their invasion, proliferating, spreading, and causing less damage than their predecessors. They eat great quantities of weed seeds and also wild and cultivated fruits. (In California the birds are a menace to cherries and figs.) So far, however, the newcomers have been well received wherever they've colonized.

Jeanne Friswell and family, of Holliston, Massachusetts, gladly took in a fledgling finch several years ago: "Fescue is a particular kind of fine grass which comes up in sprigs, so when our cat brought a baby house finch home in his mouth, 'Fescue' became his name; his head was covered with fine little wisps sticking straight up. We put Fescue in a warm cardboard box with soft grass—to die in peace. But he was a survivor, and in the morning was chirping from starvation. We fed him weed seeds mashed in baby pabulum from an eyedropper, until he became strong enough to flap around in his box.

"Fescue's chirps became louder and more insistent for more food, and soon he was strong enough to fly all over our screened-in porch. On the third day, to our astonishment, his

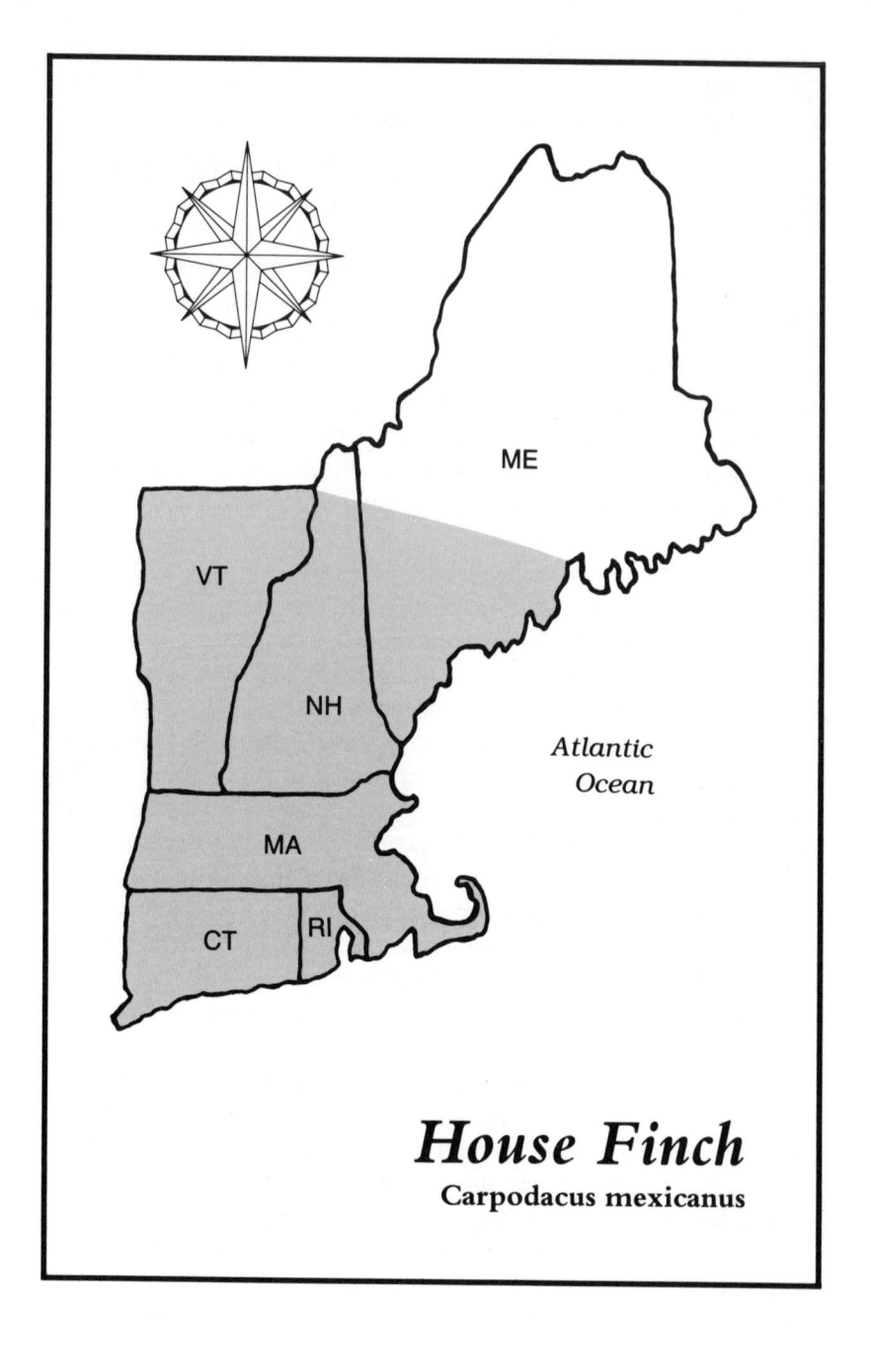

House Finch
Carpodacus mexicanus

parents recognized his calls, and flew in a frenzy all around the porch. His drab-colored mother darted repeatedly into the screen trying to reach him, while his colorful father stood guard in a bush. We put Fescue (carton and all) on the porch stairs, and as the four of us stood two feet away, the finch parents proceeded to feed their long-lost baby.

"Our two daughters were thrilled with their new 'pet' and were busy for many days collecting insects and seeds, and feeding Fescue on their fingers. Their grandfather also took his turn feeding him while we were away, and everyone helped clean the droppings scattered on the porch. We continued to put him out a couple of times a day for feedings from his parents, who did not seem to mind his newly-acquired human scent; it was as though they understood that we were all helping. In two weeks, Fescue had outgrown the porch, and we recognized the 'empty-nest syndrome' experience as we let him go—high into the trees to be with his own. Not for long! That evening, he was back on the porch roof for his supper and good old bed. This began a routine of wild and free all day, and home to roost at night. Unfortunately he didn't seem to fit in with the fine-feathered crowd, and he didn't know how to find food. He came home starving every night, and if we called him during the day, he would fly down to perch on a friendly head or shoulder for a few comforting words and a snack. Once, he sat up in a tree all night in the rain and decided 'this is for the birds,' so back he came for free room and board.

"Fescue's story does not have the proverbial happy ending; Muffy caught him again and his little life ended quickly. We buried him and were all very quiet for a few days, asking 'Why?' Would we do it all again? Of course. We all benefited from the experience: a little piece of life, a bit of nature shared. Many years from now, our girls will say, 'Remember Fescue?' "

House finches nest in a wide variety of places, including bushes, trees, cavities, desert cacti, building ledges and crannies, and inside birdboxes. The nests, built mainly by females within a week, are often completed by early April. They are composed of grasses, twigs, and debris such as string, cotton or paper. Walter Clark, of Cape Cod, enjoyed monitoring a finch family around his home during the spring of 1985: "A pair of house finches flew into our back 'farmers porch' and lighted on a hanging lantern, obviously checking it for a nesting site. However, the slanting design of the lantern was quickly determined to be unsuitable. *Then* they spotted my outdoor clock up against the wall. The female promptly brought all the grasses, etc., for her nest. Needless to say, this presented us with a small problem because the porch door leads to the garage and we had to pass under the nest. It follows that the female on the nest flew off every time we passed by. In due time I used a handmirror, finding three eggs. With the hatching, the male did his part in feeding routines. He was always nearby. I could see active heads popping up over the lip of the nest. In time, of course, they all flew off, and I was able to examine their old home. Not a sign of any shells, nor was the inner nest fouled. A very nice experience . . . and we could then pass freely to the garage!"

The three to six nestlings often do befoul their nests, but only the outer rim. Pairs raising second broods simply add a bit more nesting material to cover up the fecal deposits. The young are relatively slow growers, fed by both parents via regurgitation. They fledge in about two and a half weeks. Come late summer, young and old form flocks, searching for seeds in fields and at backyard feeders. These are hardy birds, staying put throughout winter with little or no movement toward warmer climes.

Population and Range

It has long been illegal to cage native birds, but where there's money to be made, laws are frequently broken. Such was the case with house finches. Some of the linnets were shipped from

California to Long Island in 1940 to be sold as "Hollywood Finches." Apparently, when things got too hot, the dealers released the birds to avoid stiff fines. The rest is documented history: the finches spread to New Jersey and Pennsylvania by 1955, reached Connecticut by 1958, and by the mid-60s there were tens of thousands chirping across the Northeast. Undoubtedly birdfeeders have helped their range expansion, and the species' habit of living close to humans hasn't hurt. Given the chance, and with house sparrows barely holding their own, the finches have flown high and wide with the opportunity.

They are permanent residents from Maine to the Carolinas and west to Michigan. They are also increasing in the Maritimes. It has been estimated that their numbers have increased a thousand-fold from 1950 to 1980, and their main radiating direction from point of release (New York) has been southwesterly. The only end in sight to their expansion is when they converge with original western U.S. populations, which, at the current rate, might occur within the next 20 years.

• *Journal Notes* •

May 18, 1978

I came upon a pathetic sight today at Beaver Country Day School in Brookline, Massachusetts. A male house finch was perched on its nest, dead, its head twisted to the side. Two chicks lay underneath him, and a female called plaintively nearby. The nesting site is inside of a lamp hanging from a portico ceiling, about nine feet high. I guess the bird was electrocuted by the broken (yet perhaps live) light bulb dangling right over the nest. Much too close for comfort.

Evening Grosbeak

Hesperiphona vespertina

The flashy, almost gaudy evening grosbeak is unique in the East as the only big, yellow songbird with a stout bill. Its generic name, *Hesperiphona,* is from the Greek, meaning evening singer; its specific name, *vespertina,* is Latin, also referring to the evening. Long ago, it was erroneously believed that the species sang mostly at night.

Field Guidelines

The prominent bill, white wing patches, and yellow chest and back identify the male evening grosbeak. Females are gray with touches of yellow. Both sexes show the black and white wings in an undulating type of flight. The familiar winter calls are reminiscent of a house sparrow's: loud, monotonous chirping, but with a ring to it.

Grosbeaks are mainly birds of northern coniferous forests, although most New Englanders know them at winter feeders, gobbling up fruit, hemp and sunflower seeds. Eliot Taylor remarked on their voracious appetites: "Thirty years ago, a lady in Sherborn, Massachusetts, fed as many as 80 evening grosbeaks. She told me that one year she fed them a ton and a half of sunflower seeds—at a cost of $400. On one of my visits to her house, I found that it took a grosbeak five seconds to pick up a seed, break the shell, swallow the heart, drop the case, and start on the next seed. The woman is now deceased, but many grosbeaks still return to the neighborhood feeders each year."

Other favorite foods include maple samara (especially boxelder), dogwood and cherry berries, and, like other northern finches, salt. The birds are often seen in small groups picking up road salt, and at such times are easily approached . . . or killed by cars. Stella Luster, of Antrim, New Hampshire, received an injured grosbeak once, fondly recalling the experience: "Annie, a female evening grosbeak with a broken wing that never healed, came to us in February of 1982. We had her in a cage at first, then she roamed the kitchen freely. I had a ball trying to catch her. I'd be pooped. After awhile she became used to our presence, and would take sunflower and apple seeds from my fingers. When she took a bath she really enjoyed splashing water as far as she could—all over the floor and windows. She really was a darling.

"One day during her second season with us, I realized she wasn't eating properly; she just huddled and seemed to shiver. I tried all kinds of treats (grapes especially) but she didn't re-

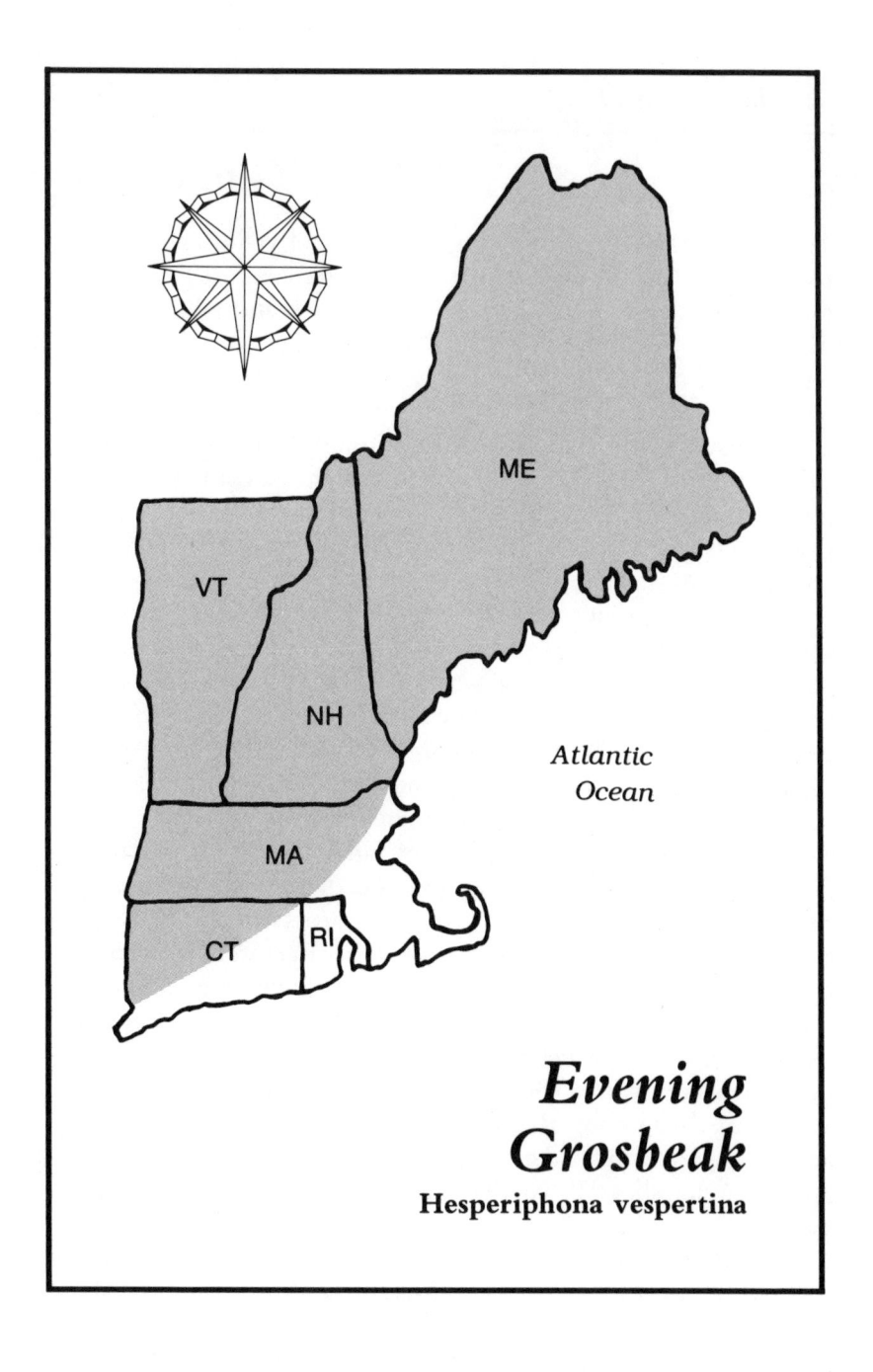

ME

VT

NH

Atlantic Ocean

MA

CT RI

Evening Grosbeak

Hesperiphona vespertina

spond. The vet gave us medication and vitamins but nothing seemed to work. Finally, after two weeks of illness, I couldn't stand to see her suffer anymore. I used some chloroform and put her to sleep, which was much easier for me to do than see her suffer. I buried Annie at the foot of a tree facing the greenhouse. I enjoyed her and so did everyone else—a little fluff of sunshine gone to rest."

It takes time, luck, and knowledge of natural history to find a grosbeak nest; they are usually placed high in a conifer and well concealed from below. Twigs sewn with moss or lichens form the base, and the lining is of fine rootlets. The three to five eggs are striking: blue-green, blotched or spotted with purple or black. They strongly resemble those of the red-winged blackbird. Following a two-week incubation period, and another two to three weeks to fledge, the young head out, flying high in grosbeak style toward other cold regions.

Norman Boucher, a writer and outdoors enthusiast from Boston, wrote of his first encounters with and impressions of these likable birds: "I first saw evening grosbeaks from taking an ornithology course at the University of New Hampshire back in 1972. While flocks of people headed south to Florida as soon as the first frost hit the Granite State, there were rumors circulating that some birds actually flew south to New Hampshire for winter relief. These were hardy birds I had to see.

"I heard them first while walking to the student union building for lunch one day, when gray clouds heavy with snow were settling in. I looked up at what sounded like someone jostling a bag of silver dollars overhead. There they were, in a hurry as they always seem to be in flight, a dozen dark birds with flashes of white and yellow. I only had a glimpse before they were gone.

"Later, at yard feeders, I saw them more closely. With that massive, frowning bill capable of destroying who knows how many sunflower seeds, and with that little yellow lightning bolt over the eye, the males appear ready for a fight, though I've never seen them do anything more than hunker down in the lilacs or deplete a feeder in record time. Their coloring, all those shades of yellow more suited to the tropics than the arctic, must be another act of defiance, a statement of the daring that brings them to the New England suburbs in winter in increasing numbers. I can never look at a grosbeak without trying to imagine their breeding range, their home, the vast stretches of tundra, where snowy owls and gyrfalcons roam, where man with his feeders and troublesome pollution are just a memory in the mysterious mind of these private birds."

Population and Range

At the turn of this century evening grosbeaks were still unknown east of the Great Lakes. Shortly thereafter they periodically straggled far eastward, and during the 1920s birds banded in Michigan were recovered in New England. Slowly, as more feeding stations sprang up, grosbeaks began lingering after winter to breed in these new areas. Boreal seed-eaters such as redpolls, crossbills, siskins, and grosbeaks erupt sporadically depending on tree seed crops; if northern spruce or birch crops fail, the birds wander east and south. And they keep moving until they find sufficient amounts of food for their large flocks, which number in the hundreds if not thousands. Weather perhaps plays a part in their movements. Without all those trays of sunflower seeds, though, the birds would surely have skipped south of New England and kept flying until they reached better natural feeding grounds.

• *Journal Notes* •

March 5, 1986

As the maple sap finally starts flowing, the evening grosbeaks continue to go through the sunflower seeds here at an alarming rate. I've noticed that they call just after dawn, high in an ash tree, waiting for me to fill the tray and tubes. These are truly gregarious birds—calling, flying, and feeding as one. The combined voices sound like distant sleigh bells, and the combined wings sound like flags in a hefty breeze. I find these motley birds both comical and endearing. I envy their roaming spirit, their boreal leanings. Perhaps some day I'll live among moose, loons, and clownish grosbeaks of far northern regions. The calls of the wild—exciting and deeply felt—must be heeded. Some day. Some old day.

Afterword

Something exciting is indeed happening around New England: birds and mammals roving where they've never been before. During the last few decades alone (with the continual decline of small farming and the gradual takeover by forests), coyotes, moose and opossums have significantly expanded their ranges. Beavers have made a startling comeback, creating new aquatic habitats for all types of living creatures. And most of the species in this book are relatively recent invaders, capitalizing on changes in land use.

Although some wildlife species have declined since World War II, others have actually increased—an amazing feat considering the widespread loss of wetlands, woods and fields to bulldozers and backhoes. Time marches on, with Progress joyriding alongside, but wildlife somehow keeps pace from a distance, adapting for sheer survival.

These are inspiring years for birdwatchers and everyone else who enjoys monitoring what's new in the woods. Each hike has the potential for real surprises, even in the familiar backyard. Anticipation hovers over stone walls and seashores on wayward wings.

Neal Clark
Hancock, NH
May, 1988

Bibliography

The following lists the major sources which helped in the preparation of this guide.

Allen, Arthur H. *The Book of Bird Life*. D. Van Nostrand Co., Inc., Princeton, New Jersey, 1961.

Bailey, Wallace. *Birds of the Cape Cod National Seashore*. Eastern National Parks and Monuments Assoc., 1968.

Beddall, B.G. Range expansion of the cardinal and other birds in the northeastern states. *Wilson Bulletin*. 75:140–158, 1963.

Bent, Arthur Cleveland. *Life Histories of North American Birds*. Government Printing Office, Washington, D.C., 1921.

Borror, Arthur C. *Breeding Birds of the Isles of Shoals*. Shoals Marine Lab., Cornell University, Ithaca, N.Y., 1980.

Graham, Frank, Jr. *Gulls—A Social History*. Random House, N.Y., 1975.

Harrison, Hal H. *A Field Guide to Birds' Nests*. Houghton Mifflin Co., Boston, 1975.

Hay, John. *The Run*. Ballantine Books, N.Y., 1959.

Martin, Alexander C., Nelson, Arnold L., and Zim, Herbert S. *American Wildlife and Plants*. Dover Publications, Inc., N.Y., 1951.

Niering, William. *The Life of the Marsh*. McGraw-Hill Book Co., N.Y., 1966.

Peterson, Roger Tory. *A Field Guide to the Birds*. Houghton Mifflin Co., Boston, 1980.

Roth, Charles E. *Walking Catfish and Other Aliens*. Addison-Wesley Publishing Co., Inc., Reading, Mass., 1973.

Stefferud, Alfred, ed. *Birds in Our Lines*. Government Printing Office, Washington, D.C., 1966.

Stokes, Donald W. *A Guide to the Behavior of Common Birds*. Little, Brown and Co., Boston, 1979.

Terres, John. *The Audubon Society Encyclopedia of North American Birds*. Knopf, N.Y., 1980.

Vickery, Peter D. *Annotated Checklist of Maine Birds*. Maine Audubon Society, 1978.

Welty, Joel Carl. *The Life of Birds*. W.B. Saunders Co., Philadelphia, 1975.

Wetmore, Alexander. *Water, Prey, and Game Birds of North America*. National Geographic Society, Washington, D.C., 1965.

NOTES

NOTES